AF510400

International Property Insurance Programmes

From Theory To Experience-based Practice

Claudio Böttcher and Andy Baumli

Expect the **unexpected** to **happen**.

First published in 2021 by Paragon Publishing, Rothersthorpe

© Claudio Böttcher and Andy Baumli, December 2021

Edited by www.proof-reading-service.com

Front cover image: Claudio Böttcher and Andy Baumli

The rights of Claudio Böttcher and Andy Baumli to be identified as the authors of this work have been asserted by them in accordance with the Copyright, Designs and Patents Act of 1988.

All rights reserved; no part of this publication may be reproduced, stored in a retrieval system, or transmitted in any form or by any means, electronic, mechanical, including scanning, photocopying, recording or otherwise without the prior written consent of the publisher or a licence permitting copying in the UK issued by the Copyright Licensing Agency Ltd.

www.cla.co.uk

ISBN 978-1-78222-901-8

Book design, layout and production management by Into Print
www.intoprint.net

+44 (0)1604 832149

Contents

Claudio Böttcher

Andy Baumli

1

Introduction

1.1 About the Writers/Authors

Claudio Böttcher, ACII, Chartered Insurer

Claudio Böttcher is an Associate of the Chartered Insurance Institute and a Chartered Insurer; he is an insurance professional with 40 years' experience in several senior executive roles related to direct international insurance and facultative reinsurance and with a focus on underwriting (mainly property and business interruption), portfolio management, training and auditing as well as in-house broking.

Over the years, he has developed strong competencies in customer orientation, networking and change management. He is well regarded and known for his leadership skills, charismatic personality, contagious optimism, strong integrity and passion for turning challenges into opportunities and finding timely, unorthodox solutions.

Claudio Böttcher is the Owner and Managing Director of **Claudio Böttcher Insurance Consulting GmbH** (www.ShareExpex.com) (boettcher@shareexpex.com).

Andy Baumli, MBA (exec.), *AGSM*

Andy Baumli is a senior executive with strong local and international insurance, reinsurance and broking business and client management experience plus expertise across all industries including multinational and local complex risks.

His business experience has been gained through such roles as international property insurance manager, marketing and business development manager, client manager, international business unit manager, project leader and change agent.

Andy Baumli is the Owner and Managing Director of **E4E Baumli Consulting** (www.ShareExpex.com) (baumli@shareexpex.com).

1.2 The Purpose of this Book

For many years, we have been thinking about putting our heads together and writing a living book about international property insurance programmes to share our combined 80+ years of experience in this field. Our aim in this book is to provide you with a comprehensive insight into and guidance through the extensive field of establishing and managing international property insurance programmes as well as an understanding of the most important aspects/parameters of underwriting complex global industrial risks. The success of your company lies within your capability to apply your fundamental knowledge to finding the right insurance solutions for your clients and to ensuring that these solutions meet their needs as well as complying with the legal and regulatory requirements in all the countries in which they operate. The target audience of this book is underwriters and risk and insurance managers as well as insurance intermediaries, college students and others with an interest in the topic.

Chapter 2 will introduce you to two fundamental principles:

1. meeting the customers' needs and
2. the underwriting risk appetite.

The combination of these two principles is crucial for the success of any insurance company. Would we focus and work on a solution solely concerning one of these aspects in a vacuum? There is a substantial chance that we would miss:

a. the target of meeting and satisfying the requirements of the customers and/or
b. the set underwriting risk appetite.

Chapter 3 follows chapter 2 seamlessly as we examine the essentials of crafting an international property insurance programme. There are various potential types/solutions that we need to consider and understand to ensure that we ultimately make the right decision. Insurance companies may compete primarily on the price, but very often the chosen concept and structure attract the attention of the customers.

Chapter 4 deals with the underwriting considerations, which are the fundamentals of a sound and professional underwriter, who must demonstrate the necessary skills at any time and on all levels. When submitting an insurance solution, we must be sure that we have considered all the possible aspects of the insurance cover and the implications for the insurance company.

Chapter 5 concerns programme handling and is linked to Chapter 3 ("potential types/solutions"), submitting some ideas about how to approach the programme structure. In contrast to Chapter 3, in which the possible options are explained, this chapter deals with the operational part once the customer and underwriter have decided which type of international property programme to put in place.

Chapter 6 handles reinsurance, in particular facultative reinsurance and spot fac., as well as the importance of concurrency.

Chapter 7 focuses on the international network: structuring the required network for handling your international property insurance programmes as well as the importance of good communication within your network.

Chapter 8 deals with risk management and the critical use of risk engineering information as well as the difference between BCM (business continuity management) and BCP (business continuity planning). It also points out why they are important in our underwriting process.

We hope that this book will be of great assistance to you and that you will enjoy reading it.

Should you have any specific questions, remarks or feedback or any input to help improve the content of this book, please feel free to share your comments with us via our landing page at **www.ShareExpex.com**.

ShareExpex

Share Experience and Expertise

Any suggestions regarding additions that you would like to see included in future editions of this book are more than welcome!

2

Getting Started

Claudio Böttcher

This chapter will introduce you to two fundamental principles. We believe that both are core elements that we need to deal with before investigating the technical underwriting aspects of setting up an international property insurance programme solution. We will just provide a conceptual description here and not enter into full details, given the great amount of literature available for the reader to refer to if needed.

These two principles are:

- The meeting the customers' needs principle
- The underwriting principle

2.1 The Meeting the Customers' Needs Principle

The ability to meet customers' needs and expectations is the key to a well-performing insurance company in the short and long term. There is more behind that simple and clear statement than it would initially seem. How often have we read similar expressions over the last decades? However, making a declaration of intent in a marketing communication is one thing and taking it from purpose to execution is another.

Forty years ago, when I started my insurance career as a young insurance manager of a retail company, my boss – the vice-chairman of the company – told me at our first meeting:

> What we need is an insurance company that understands our needs.

Such a wise and simple statement has been my companion and part of my underwriter's DNA since 1980.

This principle became more evident when I joined an insurance company in 1986 as an account executive, operating and competing in a small market with over 300 other companies. At that time, the market was highly regulated and included one monopolistic reinsurer. Policy wordings and ratings were regulated, with very little room for alternatives and exceptions. Our only option to differentiate ourselves from the competitors at that time was to strengthen our customer-centric approach, not only because of our financial strength, as we were a local branch of an international insurance company, but also, being of the upmost importance, because of our strong service capabilities. These included understanding our customers' distinctive needs from an insurance point of view, risk engineering to help mitigate and reduce potential exposures, accurate and timely policy issuance and claims handling and even, within the limitations of the regulations, the ability to respond to specific risk transfer issues.

My colleagues and I had nothing else in mind but to be competitive and to provide added value to the customer experience. Our customers were always at the centre of everything we did. We did not talk about this; **we just did it**. For us, it was a logical, natural and self-evident approach, maybe because we were young, probably because we were naive and altruistic professionals or just because this principle was the right way for us to succeed in such a competitive environment. Whatever the answer might be, I can only say that we worked with passion and energy. We embodied this principle and put all of our energy and efforts into trying to deliver what we had promised to the highest standards.

Of course, very often, we received requests for things that we were not able to provide. It goes without saying that you will not always be in a position to deliver what the customer wants, regardless of the reason – whether it is beyond your risk appetite, against the local regulations or impossible on some other grounds. It is then even more important that you are able to articulate this to your customer and, where possible, offer an alternative solution or submit another option before you communicate that you are declining the business. There is no one-size-fits-all approach to such a situation. I just want to underline the importance of proper and professional communication with your customer in any case. Explain the reasoning behind your decision in full detail.

In a nutshell, listening to what your customer wants and keeping your promises once made as well as delivering on them form the first principle that every underwriter needs to internalise deeply. You need to believe in this principle and apply it every single time you are dealing with customers because it will be the foundation on which you can build trust and a long-term relationship. Insurance is not only about people and relationships. It is also about trust. Without understanding what your customer wants and needs, you will never be able to deliver according to their expectations.

The foundation of a long-term relationship and trust is set by listening to what your customer wants and needs and then delivering on your promises. This is the first key principle that every underwriter needs to internalise deeply.

Understanding customer needs must be the driver of your behaviour in all that you do.

Today, increased competition is driving insurance companies to invest in new technologies to increase their ability to meet customer expectations. The insurance industry has improved its understanding of how to deal with customers in the way that customers want to be treated, whether this happens through a digital platform, via their broker or on a direct basis.

Customers are now much more educated and knowledgeable about insurance, not only in large corporations but also in all other segments. Offering more of the same or just retouching the heading of an extension endorsement to make it look new or refreshed is not the means of staying successful in the market. The key approach is to focus on better customer engagement and foster loyalty. A customer-centric culture throughout the whole organisation is the only strategy to ensure and achieve sustainable growth and profits in the long run. Customer demand is evolving rapidly and extends beyond an insurance policy. Customers also want services anywhere, at any time and through any channel.

“It is difficult to deal with you”. How many times have we heard this statement from our customers or brokers? Our industry has had the ability to turn very simple matters into complicated ones. Simplifying the interaction with our customers is pivotal in today’s complex world. Digitalisation seems to be the key word in every publication that we read. We need to be clear that it is only a means. It is not about **WHAT** but about **HOW** we implement and use digitalisation to simplify our processes. Whichever company you work for, the essence is to simplify customers' experience and meet their expectations. It is about responding quickly, turning their challenges into solutions and building trust through efficient delivery so that they know they can rely on you and your organisation if things go wrong.

> Digitalisation is only a means and not the medicine for an illness. Only a truly customer-centric culture including a combination of customer-related propositions and services supported by digitalisation tools will help organisations to navigate today's very crowded and competitive market.

2.2 The Underwriting Principle

Blending Art and Science?

As we know it today, underwriting can be defined in very simple terms as the process whereby an underwriter or organisation, in the following order and steps:

1. decides whether to accept the risk,
2. determines the scope of coverage as well as the terms and conditions,
3. calculates the price that is commensurate with the risk.

Let us look together at the main considerations for each step.

Step 1 – Risk Selection and Assessment

This is the first key step in the underwriting process and is the basis for deciding whether and how to use the available capacity.

Risk selection is based on the risk appetite as defined by the organisation. Typically, every insurance company will define a risk appetite matrix, which combines the severity and quality of the risk of the activity under consideration with the share and amount that it is prepared to take.

Risk assessment includes ***physical*** (objective) and ***moral*** (subjective) hazards.

Physical hazards are the hazards attached to the physical features of the risk (the subject matter of insurance). Typical features that underwriters will analyse here are, for example, whether it will cause peril in operation for an insured, increase the size of the resulting claims, hinder efforts to reduce damage or to control it or induce difficulty in the discovery of an incident. To assist underwriters with their risk assessment, they will generally require information about the following:

- The activity of the business;
- Construction and layout;
- Protection and security;
- Heating and electrical information;
- Storage and use of hazardous materials or susceptible materials;
- Adjoining premises.

In its basic approach, it involves what in the insurance industry is referred to as **COPE** information:

Construction – how the building was made;
Occupation – what the building is used for;
Protection – how the building is protected;
Exposure – external factors near the building that may expose or increase a threat.

Moral hazards are the hazards concerning the attitude of the insured. They concern the human factor that arises from the behaviour and that may increase the possibility of a loss as a consequence of carelessness or dishonesty.

Examples of the information that underwriters will require are:

- Claims history;
- Condition of the premises;
- Attitude towards risk improvement recommendations;
- Safety awareness of the customer's management.

Step 2 – Scope of coverage, terms and conditions

After risk selection and assessment, underwriters will design the account structure and coverage scope to meet the customer's needs. The policy wording, extension clauses, limits, sub-limits and deductible levels are the major elements under consideration in this step.

A considerable amount of analysis needs to be performed, in particular when bespoke wording or alien extensions, such as non-damage business interruption (NDBI) extensions, are required. Understanding the potential exposure to losses, whether in relation to their frequency or in relation to their severity, is fundamental. In addition, the geographical distribution of the insured locations and their exposure to natural, terrorism and other perils are essential to facilitate the setting of the level of limits that you are prepared to offer.

Reading policy wording of more than 60 pages is not a task that every underwriter wants to perform. More often than not, various risks that are hidden and not fully understood can expose an insurance company to severe losses. Insurance litigation is overwhelmed by unintended cover aspects, leading to substantial losses. Clarity of cover before inception remains the key for all the parties involved in the relationship – customer, broker/agent and underwriters. Contract certainty is a major requirement of the regulators in most jurisdictions worldwide, hence the importance of fully understanding the coverage that you are providing.

Step 3 – Pricing

Together with your risk assessment conclusions, the scope of coverage, terms and conditions will be the core elements of the final step – pricing.

The Concept of Technical Pricing

In general terms, the technical price reflects technical considerations such as:

- The costs of production, which will embrace small losses, large losses, catastrophic losses, expenses (direct and allocated), reinsurance expenses and the cost of the capital to achieve the insurance company's profit goals;
- The territorial scope, nature, size and risk quality of the customer's operations;

- The policy wording – all offered/bound terms and conditions together with all adjustment clauses, extensions, exclusions and wording alterations;
- The programme structure (for example limits, sub-limits and deductibles);
- The economic and legal environment (for instance inflation and statutory levels).

2.3 The Concept of Price to Market

Technical pricing sometimes has limitations as a result of possible bias in the model price, resulting in under- or overpriced conclusions. This is the time when the underwriter's experience and capabilities will play an important role in adjusting the technical price to a more realistic price for the account. When making this adjustment, underwriters should take into account not only their own knowledge and experience but also those of the customers as well as competitive considerations.

Technical pricing is not to be disregarded. It is important to understand that it only serves as a benchmark, anchor or starting point for underwriters to determine the final price for the account. It will be one of the many sources at the moment of balancing technical and commercial considerations. It will help to bring together underwriting science and art to produce a result. Very often, in the underwriter's mind, it will be like a war of considerations in opposition (technical vs commercial). The experience of the underwriter will enable a balanced outcome for the mutual benefit of the customer and the insurance company by applying common sense and prudent judgement.

All in all, technical pricing is a fundamental component driving price adequacy in a portfolio. However, it is only the starting point for the final pricing consideration of an account.

2.4 Putting the Cart before the Horse

The underwriting steps are all equally important, but underwriting must follow the right and only order of tasks to ensure sustainable performance when applied either to an individual account or to the book of business. We have seen underwriters who, due to top line management pressure, have put the cart before the horse by looking first into the pricing of an account. If the result was about or above the technical price determined by their own pricing models, this was the deciding factor for writing a risk. The quality of the risk was disregarded since the perfume of the premium was overpromising. We can only say, however, that there is no premium in the world that can compensate for poor risk quality. A poor risk remains a poor one no matter how high the premium charged for it is. This situation can become even worse when underwriters start to build property portfolios on the basis of technically well-priced accounts for less than desired or even non-acceptable risk quality accounts. Very soon, the loss activity will put the whole portfolio under pressure, resulting in performance that does not deliver sustainable results. Re-underwriting the book will be the measure taken to improve the results. Such activities will often conclude in very painful and distractive necessary activities that might end up eroding customers' and distributors' relationships. The underwriting principle (the blending of science and art) remains the critical approach for writing profitable business.

2.5 Conclusion

In this chapter, we have provided you with insights into two principles that we believe to be important to bear in mind before crafting an international property programme solution.

Meeting Customers' Needs – Understanding and listening to customers' needs is the foundation for a long-term relationship and the building of trust. Listening to what your customers want and then delivering on your promise within the realms of what is possible within your organisation (capacity and risk appetite availability) form the key principle.

Underwriting – Combining underwriting expertise, data analytics (claims statistics, risk quality and exposure information, model results, etc.) with prudent judgement, underwriting curiosity and common sense are the basis for successful underwriting.

Let us then always remember:

> Understanding and listening to customers' needs is the foundation for a long-term relationship and the building of trust through a customer-centric strategic approach.
>
> Underwriting expertise combined with prudent judgement, underwriting curiosity and common sense is the basis for successful underwriting.

3

Potential Types/Solutions

Claudio Böttcher and Andy Baumli

This chapter will introduce you to potential types/solutions for the crafting of international property insurance programmes. The following will describe some examples of these potential solutions; however, it will not cover all the alternatives that might be available. We will guide you through the most typical approaches, given that customers may have different needs based on the nature of their business activities and their risk profile regarding how they wish to resolve their insurance requirements; hence, they will need a tailor-made solution rather than a standard approach.

This chapter explains the options available, and Chapter 5 will deal with the operational details once a structure has been chosen.

3.1 What Are the Key Benefits of a Programme?

- **The expense control** (the premiums) and the potential savings associated with the insurance of all the assets belonging to the customer located around the world. These will allow customers centralised negotiation and purchasing power according to their global needs. In addition, the spread of risks around the globe has a risk diversification effect, which is generally in the overall premium.
- **A consistent and uniform scope of cover** in terms of perils, limits and deductibles. This is applicable to all the customer's companies, hence achieving an economy of scale as well as a uniform and broader coverage range, which after all provides *peace of mind to the headquarters of the group.*
- **The sharing of risks when a captive is involved.**

An important development over the last 30 years is that many large insurance companies and broking houses have increased their expertise and their capabilities to support customers not only by providing global insurance solutions but also in the servicing and handling of policy issuance, premium and tax allocation, claims management, captive and reinsurance cessions, risk engineering/management information and many others. Customers now have access to all this information through a portal via which they can download all their respective information. In some cases, the information will be available in real time since these insurers offer application programming interface (API) connectivity to their customers.

Risk managers, insurance managers and others with a similar role are now in a position to analyse trends, meet regulatory requirements, improve risk transfer processes and so on. With this technology, customers do not have to waste time pulling together reports to obtain a complete picture of their international programmes. We believe that this is an important advancement towards satisfying customer needs. Most of the large insurance groups are now able to provide these services as a standard.

While API connectivity to powerful relevant customer data might be considered an indirect benefit, we believe that this is a very important supporting criterion when deciding to set up an international property insurance programme. This is true not only for large corporations but also for companies operating in the middle market sector including some international exposure (the main facility situated in one country and operations located in, say, two or three other countries).

Additional Benefits

Do you see any additional benefits to those mentioned above? If so, would you like to share them with us for future editions of this book?

3.2 Structure Examples

3.2.1 Single Policy

Following this approach, all the worldwide property exposures would be insured under one single policy. However, such a policy would be challenging to manage and operate. We do not believe that there are any such policies currently in place. This type of policy was a practice in the London market in the 1970s and early 1980s.

The benefit of the simplicity of a single policy is overturned by the following facts:

- In many countries, local regulations and legislation may prohibit the insurance of local exposures/risks outside the country (non-admitted insurance);
- It prevents the flow of money (premium and claims) in or out of the country;
- Severe penalties may be imposed if acting against local legislation. It is to be noted that not only the involved insurance company but also the customer and the intermediary might face sanctions;
- Other implications involve a loss of tax allowances if the premium is not paid locally, and it will be extremely difficult to perform a loss adjustment in these countries without having a local policy.
- The cross-border capital flow to settle a local loss may be hindered by local regulations or even sanctioned.

This approach is not the recommended way to handle global exposures, and we have a clear view about and position against such an irresponsible solution. The reason for mentioning it here is to make you aware of the risks and consequences of such a methodology.

3.2.2 Local Policies Only

Alternatively, local policies could be issued in each country, but again customers would not benefit from the advantages of expense control and potential savings as well as a consistent and uniform scope of cover. These may lead to a gap in the cover, higher insurance premiums due to the lack of spreading of risk and the possible application of the underinsurance clause.

3.2.3 Local Policies and a Master Policy

In our view, the most customer-focused approach to arranging international cover is to combine a master policy, typically issued in the country where the customer is headquartered, with supporting local policies issued in the countries where the customer is located. This is the simplest method for setting an international programme. There will be occasions when a variation to the approach will be needed, as might be the case when it is necessary to implement financial interest cover (FinC; see Chapter 4.3.8). In addition, there are certain aspects of cover that are generally handled under the master policy only (e.g., extensions such as interdependency). We will refer to these points in more detail in Chapter 4.

In essence, the operation of this structure involves the following:

- The master policy will set out the full global cover agreed with the customer centrally.
- Local policies will be issued that are as close as possible to the master policy in relation to coverage, terms and conditions.
- The master policy will provide for difference in conditions (DIC) and/or difference in limits (DIL) when a local policy is issued using purely local standards and market practices and therefore cannot fully respond to the agreed broader coverage and higher limits under the master policy (see also Chapter 4.3.7).
- The premiums will in general reflect the extent of the coverage provided locally. There might be occasions when the local premium will reflect the extent of the cover provided by the master and local policies where this is legally possible. In this case, it might be feasible to benefit from the full deduction of the premium for tax allowances.

3.3 Compliant Programmes

Regulations and legislation applicable to international property programmes have already been in place for many years. However, in our experience in this field, we have observed that regulations at the global level have undergone important changes in the last couple of decades. These involve many aspects affecting insurance requirements, such as coverage, licences, capitalisation and solvency requirements as well as premium taxation and others:

- Many regulators have arrangements with other regulators and tax authorities in place whereby they can exchange information.
- As a result of the above, a greater focus is put on global companies by, for example, tax authorities, which control those taxes on affected premiums that are paid locally.
- Cases such as Kvaerner plc v. Staatsecretaris van Fiancien (2001) in the European Union as well as other cases in Argentina and Switzerland have stressed this continuous regulatory control trend.

These cases have provided evidence that the legal requirements today are more than just a paragraph stated in a regulation or tax legislation.

- Society has changed its view of compliance from one in which regulatory and tax compliance is purely a legal need to one in which it is just good business practice and governance. This is a positive trend as it is also seen in the corporate world as a requirement (or demand) for sustainability and image gain as well as participation and diversity.
- Corporate reputation and responsibility seem to have a greater weight than in the past. Companies include this aspect as a serious part of their risk management approach and take measures to avoid litigation or negative press. The coronavirus (COVID-19) pandemic, during which companies have undertaken all possible measures to protect their employees and their company name by doing the right thing, serves as a good example here.
- In many cases, shareholders, analysts and other interested parties (including non-profit organisations) require companies to provide a guarantee of compliance with all applicable regulations and legislation.

To help you to understand the potential areas affected, here, we provide a list of the most common ones based on our empirical observations over the years. It should be noted that this is not a full and complete list (of issues and countries) as this is a dynamic area and changes can happen as we speak. Therefore, they need to be taken into consideration and updated on a regular basis.

- Non-admitted insurance is one of the oldest aspects included in the regulations. For some countries, this is absolutely forbidden; for others, it is allowed but subject to taxation on the affected premium. In addition, there are cases in which non-admitted insurance is allowed once it has been offered first in the local market and refused to be taken up by local insurers.
- Local insurance taxation, including VAT, reinsurance tax, fire brigade charges, stamp duty and other types, is required in many countries.
- There are some requirements to have local representation or an applicable licence that would allow an insurance company to insure the local risk. This may include a restriction on a local insurer

reinsuring the risk to a company that does not have a licence for it.

- Coverage for specific risks, such as terrorism, natural perils and certain political risks, may only be provided by the local country insurance schemes or pools if there is a locally issued policy.
- There are requirements in some countries regarding mandatory reinsurance cessions to a state-controlled reinsurer.
- Policy forms, deductibles schemes and rates might have to be filed locally.
- While, during the last decades, many local tariffs have been disbanded or deregulated, there are still some countries where a compulsory tariff is applied to specific perils (e.g., earthquakes).

The key aspect for you to know when writing international property programmes is the importance of not only viewing situations from your own perspective within the border of your own country but also looking ahead and beyond this point of view. This is very much the case because what you can do in your country may be forbidden or not applicable in another country or countries.

3.4 How To Set Up a Compliant International Property Programme

To make such a programme compliant, the following points need to be considered as a minimum. Please note that these features are of a general nature and that each international property programme has to be viewed on its own merits.

- Local policies are to be issued as required by the respective country's law and regulations. The limits, deductibles and scope of coverage can reflect the terms and conditions agreed under the master policy but only to the extent of what is legally permitted locally.
- The premium allocation has to follow a transparent procedure not only regarding the risks in each country but also relative to the local policy conditions as well as to the master policy. In particular, for countries where DIC and DIL are allowed, taxation on this part of the premium is important for further local payment.
- Financial interest cover might be possible in certain jurisdictions. Where the parent company holds shares or any other financial

interest in the local company, this extension provides cover against the risk of the devaluation of such shares or financial interest as a result of the local company incurring property loss or damage. In other words, the insurable interest of the parent company is the resulting devaluation of the shares or financial interest in the local company and not the loss to the local assets. This extension is sometimes used when non-admitted insurance is forbidden locally and the programme insurer has neither a local representation or an applicable licence to write business in that country. We will explain this point in more detail in Chapter 4.

- Territorial scope: many countries have issued trade and economic sanctions. These are applicable to countries, goods or services and persons (individuals, institutions, entities, charities, marine vessels, aircraft, etc.). The insurance provided under your international property programme must be aligned with these requirements, as explained in Chapter 4.

3.5 Captives

Andy Baumli

Have You Ever Heard of Captives as an Alternative Insurance Solution Vehicle?

International reinsurance captives have become a major player in the industrial insurance business marketplace. Considering what they provide their owners with, it is no surprise that companies are now investigating the possibility of creating/establishing their own risk-pooling vehicle. Captives, by their nature, are an interesting, valuable alternative to the traditional straightforward insurance and reinsurance solutions. When I first heard about captives in a workshop at the headquarters of the Zurich Insurance Group, I was fascinated by the sophisticated technicality and almost inexhaustible possibilities for structuring and managing single exposures, a complete line of business or an entire risk portfolio in an effective as well as an efficient way.

Hugh Rosenbaum compiled a timeline of captives to the present. The early days (prior to 1984) of captives were dominated by very large single-parent captives and a few large group captives. They were formed in reaction to insurance crises (i.e., a lack of capacity and high prices). A do-it-yourself atmosphere prevailed in which service companies were starting to address these concerns. Tax deductions of premiums were generally not available to captive owners, and other initiatives detrimental to captives were instigated by the Internal Revenue Service (IRS). By the end of this period, the total number of captives had grown to an estimated 1,950.

The period from 1985 to 2005 was characterised by an increase in the number of captives, particularly US-based group captives. There was a rise in the number of large insurers' and reinsurers' captive "desks". On the downside, unrelated business created losses for many captives. Tax issues took centre stage, and taxpayers started winning cases. Meanwhile, the regulatory pressures began to mount. During this period, the total number of captives rose from an estimated 2,000 to 4,881.

From 2006, the amount of micro-captives, cell structures and pooling increased. Taxpayers continued to gain the upper hand in cases in the United States and in Europe. However, regulatory pressures such as Solvency II and the NAIC's risk-based measures occupied the spotlight, resulting in higher costs for captive owners. Meanwhile, the number of captives increased to more than 7,000 (A.M. Best estimate) worldwide. While Bermuda, the Cayman Islands, Barbados and Guernsey have historically been the most popular domiciles for captive formations, other locations, such as Delaware, the Isle of Man, Malta, Switzerland, Ireland, Luxembourg, Gibraltar and Singapore, also harbour captives.[1]

Why would a company contemplate the founding of a risk-caring vehicle? Self-insuring through a captive is today a common and cost-effective way of protecting companies' assets. There is, of course, also a downside in that property, casualty, workers' compensation, marine and other captives all carry a considerable amount of risk. Captives are cost effective and bear other benefits, which we will explore in more detail, but they can pose the risk of potential insolvency under certain circumstances, which companies need to be aware of before starting the process. A strong and sound capital base is inevitably the basic requirement.

A captive is a legal entity and is commonly described and defined as an insurance and reinsurance company that is wholly owned and controlled by its insured's parent company. The main purpose is to cover some or all lines of insurance, depending on the risk profile and risk appetite of the group, and to benefit from its own sound understanding of the internal and external risk environment and source of potential exposures and interruptions. The strategy set and the linked dedicated philosophy of managing the risk portfolio professionally also provide the benefit of participating in any underwriting profits.

There is no real differentiation from a traditional mutual insurance company. A mutual insurance company is by nature owned and more or less controlled by its policyholders, the insureds. Policyholders do not invest any assets in the mutual insurance company besides the insurance premium and do not actively participate in running it.

Captive insurance is utilised by companies of almost all sizes that choose:

- to manage their own risk portfolio;
- to access the international reinsurance markets directly;
- to put their own capital at risk, especially in a zero-interest environment;
- to achieve their risk-financing objectives;
- to use their own insurance expertise and experience as well as risk management.

These five essential features of a captive will provide an understanding of the nature of a captive vehicle. Other purposes of a captive are the following:

- to provide broader coverage than the traditional insurance marketplace;
- to stabilise insurance pricing and underwriting capacity;
- to improve the cash flow;
- to control the premium flow;
- to increase the control over the entire insurance programme and claims handling.

Let us discuss this point in more detail.

3.5.1 Broader Coverage and Underwriting Capacity

When faced with a big claim or a major insurance market event, such as a natural catastrophe, disease pandemic, terror or cyber-attack, political turmoil or another unpredicted event, such as 9/11 or the port blockage in the Suez Canal, the affected insurance cover may no longer be available or it may be reduced, be limited and/or have a much higher price. Many captives are therefore also established because of a lack of trust of the insurance industry in respect of coverage, to overcome local market practices and restrictions or because of the market pricing as well as an economical scale of expenses and costs. It is a fact that, very often, insurance companies tend to change their underwriting capacity deployment philosophy, structure and segmentation based on individual loss experiences or claims experience on an entire book of business or on unpredictable events to the disadvantage of the insured companies. That is exactly where a captive can successfully provide coverage for difficult and unique risks on a stable basis and can follow the strategic risk direction of the group. This is easily said, but, then again, it is important to note that adequate underwriting skills and appropriate risk management are a necessity.

For example, companies operating in heavier classes of business, such as those in the mining sector, face many challenges during their lifespan, such as softer commodity markets, cost management challenges, access to financing and increasing expectations regarding social, economic and environmental engagement with host communities and regulators. They have also been particularly hard hit by claims related to natural catastrophes, strikes and riots, equipment failure, fires and floods, which have resulted in underwriters around the globe becoming more selective in the risks that they will consider and markets becoming more reluctant to write any new business unless it is "adequately priced", thereby leading to substantially higher rates and unpredictable availability of underwriting capacity. In such industries, in which losses may be few but significant, the establishment of a captive imposes itself.

As already mentioned, the appetite of an insurance company may vary from one year to another and can lead to underwriters being forced to reduce the risk profile of the underwriting portfolio, to seek increases in the pricing and deductibles and to reduce the policy limits, thereby making it harder for members of the heavier classes to obtain full capacity with the right terms and conditions. In the past, excess of loss capacity was easier to obtain not only for the insured but also for the insurers. However, it is now becoming scarcer, leading to more substantial percentage rate increases. Today, we can see more and more insurers exiting from thermal coal mining and power generation due to the type of commodity, whether the operations are on the surface or underground and whether cover enhancements are being charged for, which were previously given as part of negotiations or as a commercial decision. Furthermore, underwriters face stricter underwriting rules and guidelines and therefore need much more underwriting information to write a risk than before.

In particular, the quality of renewal information, including responses to engineering survey risk assessment and recommendations as well as risk rating per site, is of foremost importance in the consideration of the continuation of the cover. Furthermore, as an underwriter, the extent of policy coverage, including policy limits and sub-limits, not to mention the exposure to natural catastrophe perils, plays a crucial role in the underwriting process as much as the basis of business interruption. The claims experience most likely reflects the nature of the business and provides a tendency to make risk management improvements. With the declaration of the insured values, the big question of whether they are adequate very often arises, in particular for the chosen BI cover and in respect of the coinsurance clause imposed in the contract.

The level of deductible and self-insured retention (SIR) gives a clear picture of the client's (insured's) commitment to professional risk management and understanding of the risk exposures. For the placement of the reinsurance programme of a captive, this aspect has a great influence on the pricing and capacity requirement.

An interesting observation of the global insurance market is that the shareholding also plays an important role; for example, having a US shareholder would make companies attractive to US markets, which tend to be more competitive than international markets – similar to Chinese markets. Today, the question of whether long-term relationships with key programme leaders still has an impact may differ from one insurer to another.

3.5.2 Stability Insurance Pricing

It is important not only to be able to budget the inflow of premiums and capital requirements to service the captive but also to consider the financial costs, especially the insurance costs and return on capital, which may vary substantially from one year to the next based on the overall performance and/or segment of an insurance company as well as global developments. As a captive matures and expands its own risk retention capability through sound risk management and underwriting profits, more capital is accumulated by the mother company, and the captive insurer's ability to retain risk almost independently from changes in the local or global insurance market is greater.

3.5.3 Improved Cash Flow/Control of Premium Flow

For any company, a healthy cash flow is rudimental for its survival and thus a key element of a successful captive. Cash flow improvements can be achieved in a number of ways, and the most important aspect is that losses retained through a captive reduce or eliminate underwriting profits but that reduced losses increase them. Therefore, captive insurance offers financial incentives for effectively controlling losses and managing risks. There is no doubt that safety and loss control attracts a higher level of focus and attention.

The underwriting profits and gains from the invested premiums, which would otherwise be held by a conventional insurer, are retained by the captive. Even with conservative investment portfolios, the dollar amounts are substantial due to the high levels of capital and surplus typically held.

Last but not least, the cash flow is improved by reducing the expense factors associated with insurance. The combined ratio of an insurance company is a measure of profitability used to gauge how well it is performing in its daily operations. The combined ratio is calculated by taking the sum of incurred losses and expenses and then dividing them by the earned premium. Generally, insurers allocate 60 to 70 per cent of the received premiums to loss payments, while the other 40 to 30 per cent covers expenses and profits. Captives have, by their nature, lower running costs and overheads than insurance companies, which means that, for every USD10 million in the net written premium, an estimated saving of USD1 million to USD2.5 million can be achieved by a successful operating captive in expenses alone: another plausible reason to consider a captive solution.

3.5.4 Increased Control over the Entire Insurance Programme and Claims Handling

A further benefit of a captive is undoubtedly the control over the entire insurance programme as well as the in-house control of the claims handling. When you are in the driving seat, you control the destination, speed, risk and fuel. As the owner, you are not limited to a nominal percentage share in the company's surplus but have much more: a captive is the owner of the company's strategic business purpose.

The risk management and loss control services established by the risk manager of a captive can be tailored to each insured's individual needs, resulting in a more favourable loss experience. Claims handling services are focused strictly on the rules and guidelines drafted and enforced by the captive, eliminating any possible self-directed interest that an insurance company may have.

The insurance concept, programme structure – Chapter 3 will outline the potential types – and solutions are clearly dictated by the captive's requirements for the successful implementation and management of the set strategic goals to achieve independency in the area of coverage, stability, pricing, handling and, not least, profitability.

3.5.5 Summary

In some ways, a captive insurance company resembles a mutual insurance company. However, the owner(s) of a captive place their own capital at risk, and they directly control their insurer. Captive insurance company owners are willing to risk their own capital in anticipation of the financial rewards associated with better control over their insurance programme. These include broader coverage, stabilised pricing, the availability of insurance and an improved cash flow.

The types of captive structures and rule of thumb for the minimal annual premium for the sake of choosing the right type are presented in the table overleaf.[2]

Type of captive	Description	Minimum annual premium
Single parent	Wholly owned subsidiary of the parent company; structured to meet individual company needs and potentially third-party risk at the discretion of the management.	USD1.2 million in annual premium
Multiple parent	Jointly owned by a group of companies in the same industry. Also called a group captive or homogeneous captive.	USD500K in annual premium
Heterogeneous	Jointly owned by companies of similar sizes but in different industries – also called an association captive. Companies pool resources together to form an insurance joint venture.	USD500K in annual premium
Rent-a-captive	For companies in the same industry that are not large enough to form their own captive but want the opportunities that owning a captive provides. They do not pool risk but instead pay the captive owner a fee.	As little as USD250K in annual premium – depending on the domicile
Segregated cell	Similar to a rent-a-captive in which the owner of the cell facility owns the insurance licence and runs the day-to-day management. Each cell is legally segregated from the others so that insurance risks, liabilities, assets and other pertinent information are not shared.	As little as USD250K – depending on the domicile

3.5.6 How Does a Captive Work?

The graphic below illustrates generically how captive insurance companies work and how money flows between the parent, the fronting company, the captive and the reinsurance company. As you can see, the "fronting" company is just a pass through and the captive – like a typical insurance company – uses a reinsurance company to provide excess coverage for unexpected and/or high claim losses.

The structure may differ based on the nature of the business and/or the clients' need.[3,4]

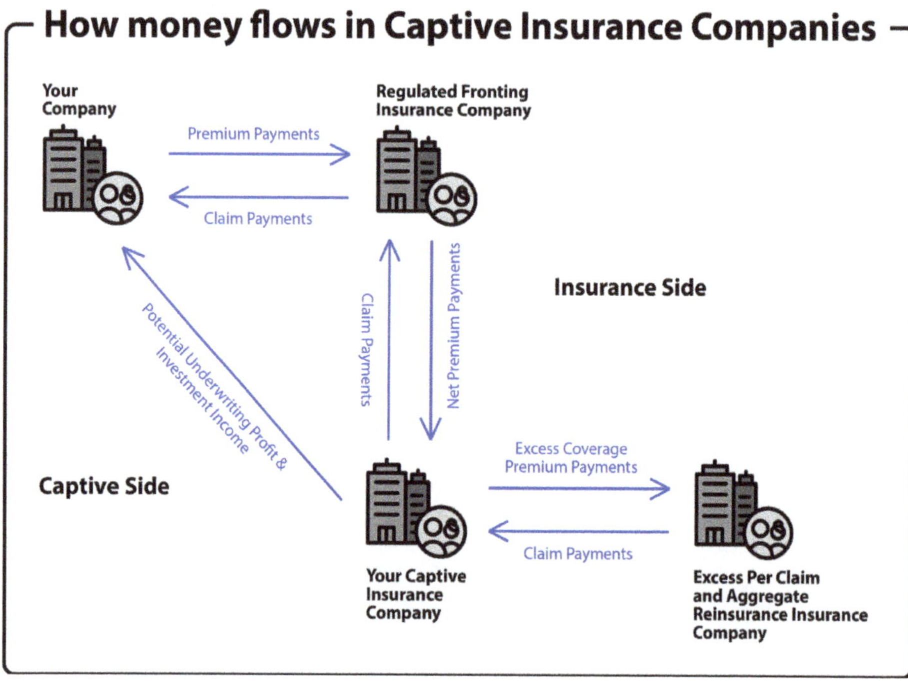

While the specifics of an arrangement may vary, a captive insurance structure frequently involves the captive owner's operating company paying premiums to a ceding or fronting company, which is a term that describes the insurance company that underwrites the captive insurance policy or "writes the paper". The company that writes the paper issues the actual insurance policy to the business that is purchasing coverage, the insured. The captive then generally reinsures the fronting or ceding company through a common type of agreement called a "quota share agreement". A quota share agreement is a pro rata reinsurance contract in which the insurer and the reinsurer share premiums and losses according to a fixed predetermined percentage.

For example, if the fronting or ceding company shares 10 per cent of the risks, it then retains 10 per cent of the premiums. If an insured pays USD2 million in premiums to a fronting or ceding company, USD200,000 would initially be retained or held back by the fronting or ceding company for claims. The remaining USD1.8 million would be transferred to the captive insurance company that is reinsuring 90 per cent of the risk from the fronting or ceding company.

A question that is often posed by captive owners is "What happens after the captive receives its premiums from the fronting or ceding company?" After all the claims have been paid, the captive's profits become part of its surplus. Surplus funds (assets minus liabilities) may be invested pursuant to the approved investment policy of the jurisdiction where the captive is licensed and governed. Importantly, surplus funds are also used to determine an insurance company's economic strength or viability and are used in many financial ratios to analyse an insurance company's viability.

A captive is a licensed, regulated entity that must qualify within a jurisdiction as an insurance company and must comply with the applicable rules and regulations. Like any business, a captive investor and shareholder enter into a transaction to earn a profit and retain the important ability to manage the operating company's risks. Once profitable, dividends are generally available within the purview of the department of insurance and its regulatory scheme for shareholders. As a licensed and regulated company, a captive insurance company will require additional care and attention over many businesses, but a captive's unique ability to manage risks and create profits for its owners can transform a business's insurance from merely a cost into a methodology for making risk management profitable.[5]

3.5.7 Underwriting Considerations

Last but not least, when I had to deal with a captive submission, I was impressed not only by the extensive technical risk underwriting skills required but also by the skills that are needed beyond the common ones to select a risk and that have different natures, such as:

- Analysing the financial statements (e.g., balance sheet, loss and profit, etc.) of a captive company;
- Drafting a "hold harmless agreement" between the insurer and the mother company of the captive to ensure that the mother company secures the self-retention of its captive vehicle in the case of a claim;
- Setting up an effective and efficient programme structure to support a smooth premium and claims payment flow, including of course the tax payments;
- Understanding the legal requirements in the set-up of the captive: which lines of business are covered by the captive, where the captive is domiciled and who is responsible for the management and who for the administration.

4

Underwriting Considerations

This chapter will provide you with an overview of a number of underwriting considerations. This section will not cover the basic technicalities of property damage and business interruption insurance as there is a large bibliography dealing with these aspects in much more detail, which we do not want to repeat here. We would rather provide you with some additional insights, based on our personal experience and observations over time, into a number of common issues that you may face when crafting an international property programme.

4.1 Property Damage Section

Andy Baumli

4.1.1 Named Perils

A Peril is a Chance Event that is Unexpected and Accidental

"Named perils" have not changed in the last hundred years. What has changed dramatically is the complexity, classes of business and technological environment affecting the changed nature of exposures. Let us have a look at the following example. The vegetarian and vegan food market has been booming over the last years, resulting in proportional growth in the number of production facilities around the world. At first glance, it would seem obvious that these factories are less risky from a property underwriting point of view. Interestingly enough, the available data do not indicate a significant difference in risk profile. Many large companies and corporations moving into the production of vegetarian and vegan products very often do so using the existing plant and machinery of their traditional food products. As a fact of the growing alternative food market, smaller enterprises are bought or replaced by larger companies and facilities. The result is a higher degree of production process automation and a greater demand for large warehouses and cold and deep-freeze stores.

The industrial technologies and processes adopted in the manufacturing of alternative foods, as well as the transport components, packaging, packaging materials and others, do not differ significantly from those used in the traditional food market. The difference lies in the use of the ingredients. Therefore, there are no significant changes to the frequency and severity of material damage. Having said that, in the context of material damage, business interruption represents a special challenge. Product freshness, including delivery and acceptance obligations, is crucial. In addition, the relocation of production lines to other companies, for example contractors, is more complex and arguably more difficult to implement due to the large number of recipes, the required quality of the products and the necessary specialised expertise. It goes without saying that the production of vegetarian and vegan food today should not be underestimated as involving lower risk by property underwriters operating in this market segment.

Digitalisation has led property underwriters to rethink the "named perils" in the traditional aspect of cover. A fire arising from a machinery explosion was and still is covered by a commercial property insurance policy excluding the machine causing the damage. How easy was that to capture and understand? With the speedy technological development, the complexity of wording interpretation has increased proportionally and is best shown by the following extract from a property insurance contract:

> Fire/Explosion
>
> Loss, damage, destruction, distortion, erasure, corruption or alteration of digital assets (to the extent they exist as electronic data and only in that form) from any cause whatsoever including but not limited to computer virus or loss of use, reduction in functionality, cost, expense of whatsoever nature (including but not limited to cyber extortion payments) and any business interruption losses resulting therefrom, regardless of any other cause or even contributing concurrently or in any other sequence to the loss.
>
> However, loss at or damage to digital assets which is the direct consequence of a physical loss or damage to other property insured by this policy by a peril listed below shall be covered and, in the event that a peril listed below results, this policy, subject to all its terms, conditions and exclusions will cover such resulting physical loss or damage.

Listed Perils:

Fire

Explosion

Loss, damage or consequential loss, additional expenditure or extra expenses of whatsoever nature directly or indirectly caused by or contributed to by or consisting of or arising in whole or in part from the way in which any data processing system responds or deals with or fails to respond to or fails to deal with any true calendar date of any data processing system respond to our dealing in any way with:

a) any data denoting a calendar date or dates as if such data did not denote a calendar date or dates, or

b) any data not denoting a calendar date or dates as if such data denoted a calendar date or dates, whether such data processing system is the property of the insured or not.

Costs expenses or fees incurred in the pursuit of system compliance or the temporary protection and or preservation of the property insured from the effects of any potential or actual failure to accomplish system compliance whether of a preventative or remedial nature or otherwise and whether incurred prior to of after any loss or damage.

I shall never forget the long hours and days reading, correcting, editing, adjusting and of course revoking a standard broker manuscript with more than 100 additional clauses to be included in the wording. To accomplish such an extensive exercise, I realised the importance not only of capturing the content of a submission but also of understanding the nature and the risk profile of the client. An insured peril in its context may have a different impact on the risk exposure from one client to another and from one industry to another. It can be said that the time of insurance product generalisation – one product for all – is clearly over and we, as underwriters, must move with the speed and complexity of actual developments.

4.1.2 Natural Perils

Of the ten costliest natural disasters in 2020, six occurred within the United States. The most destructive event was a Category 4 hurricane, Laura, which made landfall on 27 August near Lake Charles in western Louisiana with winds of 240 km/h. Hurricane Laura caused substantial wind and storm surge damage and triggered widespread flooding that extended far inland. Overall losses came to USD 13bn, with insured losses of USD 10bn.[6]

In my function as the Property Manager of an international insurance company in Australia, I still remember the day when I received a phone call from a local broker to inform me about a large claim in the Philippines. I could not believe what I heard. An unexpected strong gusty wind, with the force of almost a wind storm, smashed a crane into another crane on the harbour cargo dock in Manila and derailed, causing property damage of AUD1.5 million and business interruption of AUD 6.0 million. Manila is known to be exposed to wind storms, and I was fully aware of this fact. Before writing the international property programme, I had instructed a risk engineer to conduct a risk survey in Manila. Based on the survey report, the underwriting submission and the claims experience, I was very comfortable taking the lead on this worldwide property insurance programme. The survey report as well as my discussions with the risk manager of the insured company group convinced me that the local company in the Philippines had all the necessary precautions and measurements in place to ensure that, in the case of a wind storm, the individual cranes are pushed together and anchored at the base. The port authorities and the port operator (client) work very closely with the local bureau of meteorology, and any slight sign of an upcoming wind storm is reported immediately to enable the appropriate precautions, as mentioned above, to be taken. Unfortunately, the gusty wind did not register on the radar screen and therefore was not reported accordingly to the client. The strong gusty wind came out of the blue and hit just the one crane with full force. Even with all possible available underwriting information, data and survey reports, I was unable to predict and avoid the claim. Looking back, I should have excluded "gusty winds" as an insured peril. That was the biggest claim during my entire career as a property underwriter.

Flash Flooding/Overland Flooding

To Put It Simply, Flooding is Water Where It Is Not Wanted.

When I read the first insurance policy wording drafted in Australia, I was puzzled to read a clause called "Overland Flooding". It was my boss who shed light on the matter by explaining that overland flooding, otherwise known as flash flooding, can occur almost anywhere there is a relatively short, intense burst of rainfall, for instance during a thunderstorm. As a result, the drainage system has insufficient capacity or time to cope with the downpour, and the ground may be as hard as concrete due to a long-lasting drought and unable to absorb the water. Although flash floods are generally localised, they pose a significant threat because of their unpredictability and normally short duration.

The most costly summer for floods in Australia was 2010–11, with extensive flooding in the Lockyer Valley, Ipswich and Brisbane in January 2011. This flooding resulted in a cost of AUD6.64 billion (2013 Australian dollars, including deaths and injuries but excluding most indirect losses). In November 2011, the Australian Government introduced a standard definition of a flood for certain insurance policies. For this purpose, a flood is defined as:

> The covering of normally dry land by water that has escaped or been released from the normal confines of: any lake, or any river, creek or other natural watercourse, whether or not altered or modified; or any reservoir, canal, or dam.

Floods can have both positive and negative impacts. They can bring welcome relief for people and ecosystems suffering from prolonged drought but are also estimated to be the most costly form of natural disaster in Australia.

While the insurance cover should reflect the asset and rebuild values, it is crucial to understand the breadth and depth of the various natural perils (catastrophe risks) and exposures and therefore encourage companies to develop a robust disaster plan that takes into account the consequences of an event beyond just property damage and business interruption, such as the operational and reputational issues affecting a company in the future. Companies also need to consider how the disruption of the supply chains or distribution networks could affect the business on a worldwide basis. Companies should therefore be fully aware of any exclusions listed in the master policy and/or the local insurance policies and speculate how important these exclusions could be on their balance sheet.

Catastrophes occur at the intersection of an extreme event with a concentrated exposure. In insurance, we typically mean a single event that generates a large number of claims. To quantify the expected outcome and surrounding uncertainty of these events, catastrophe models (cat. models) have become a useful tool, even to the extent that insurance regulators in various countries specify some capital parameters in terms of catastrophic event return periods (e.g., the top limit of a cat. programme).

There is no doubt, that with the increasing number of catastrophic events and exposures, the risk transfer must be managed and transferred within and beyond the global insurance sector. Retrocession and securitisation allow for risk sharing with other financial institutions and the broader financial market, especially for the capitalisation of companies and catastrophic risk, by providing additional underwriting capacity through cat. bonds.

Swiss Re Institute sigma research reports that the insured losses from natural catastrophes and man-made disasters in 2018 amounted to USD85 billion, the fourth-highest single year total on record. While there were no mega disasters like the 2017 hurricanes Harvey, Irma and Maria, secondary perils wreaked considerable havoc and increased significantly in 2018.[7]

Lacking a formal definition, the industry considers secondary perils as high-frequency, low-to-medium-severity loss events, such as hailstorms, flash floods, tornadoes, landslides, drought and wildfires. Many times, these events appear as secondary effects of primary natural perils, such as tropical cyclone-induced flooding, liquefaction and landslides resulting from earthquakes.

Secondary perils are increasingly becoming primary drivers of losses. In 2018, nearly 62% of all natural catastrophe-related insurance claims were caused by secondary perils and secondary effects of primary perils. In the last 2 years, these perils have contributed to more than 50% of insured losses as well being responsible for some severe nat. cat. losses (e.g., flooding induced by Hurricane Harvey (2017) in Houston and the record Camp Wildfire losses (2018) in California, severe flood resulting from Cyclone Debbie (2017) in Australia and record severe flood losses in Western Japan (2018) amplified by Typhoon Prapiroon). In some countries, like Australia, secondary perils have historically been the main driver of natural catastrophe losses.

Unlike primary perils, secondary perils can largely occur anywhere; for example, torrential rainfall and the resulting flooding can happen far away from flood plains or coastal regions. This makes rapid urbanisation even more vulnerable to secondary perils. The expanding areas of paved surfaces result in rainwater running and rising along these hard surfaces instead of being absorbed into the ground.

Further, the world is becoming warmer, creating drier surface conditions and increasing the risks of wildfire outbreaks and droughts. Precipitation patterns are also changing, contributing to increased tropical cyclone-induced precipitation and severe storm surges due to the rising sea level.

Traditionally, natural catastrophe insurance and pricing for catastrophe risks was mostly influenced by the loss impact of primary perils. The experience from the past shows that the insured losses from secondary events can be significant. This means that re-/insurers need to enhance their risk assessment, monitoring and modelling tools and develop strategies to overcome the complexities of secondary peril risk assessment and modelling.

What About the Netherlands, Known as a Country Prone to Floods?

The Netherlands

When talking about floods, the Netherlands is the country that immediately comes to mind. While the country is densely populated, approximately two-thirds of its area is vulnerable to flooding due to its low elevation. On that basis, you would expect that the population would leave in fear. As an underwriter, I would be worried when flood cover is required within an international property insurance programme. Surprisingly, the latest survey shows that:[8]

A large majority of the Dutch population is confident the authorities will be able to protect the country from future flood risks.

In fact, the Dutch Government has achieved a great deal since the 1995 extreme high water levels in the rivers Rhine, Meuse and Waal, which forced some 250,000 people in Gelderland, Overijssel and Limburg out of their homes in the largest post-war evacuation of people in the Netherlands. I wonder, then, what the situation is for me as a property underwriter?

Let us have a look at the city of Rotterdam, which is the home of Europe's largest port. At 12,500 ha and with over 450 million tons of cargo being processed there every year, the Port of Rotterdam is a vibrant centre of business and a major pillar not only of the Dutch economy but also of the rest of Europe. The port's location in the Dutch delta on the North Sea makes it extremely vulnerable to floods. Rising sea levels have the potential to increase this vulnerability and not only endanger lives and goods but also affect the global economy; for us underwriters, they create the potential for big claims. At first glance, my reaction would be to keep away from such an extreme exposure, but, after completing a deeper analysis of the area and my underwriting risk assessment, I found that the authorities at the port have advanced protection mechanisms in place, such as the world's largest storm surge barrier, called the Maeslantkering. Information such as this helped me to understand the exposure of this particular location better when I was underwriting a global account.

Other precautionary measurements and defences that exist naturally and/or are undertaken by the government in the Netherlands to mitigate the risk of flood include the following:

- Natural sand dunes and constructed dikes, dams and floodgates – against storm surges from the sea.
- River dikes preventing flooding from water flowing into the country through the major rivers Rhine and Meuse.
- The complicated system of drainage ditches, canals and pumping stations, traditionally windmills of course, which keeps the low-lying parts dry for habitation and agriculture. Water control boards are the independent local government bodies responsible for maintaining this system.

I realised that everything comes back to understanding the functionality, the quality, the maintenance standards and obligations and the level of risk mitigation measures that have been undertaken and carried out by the government in the Netherlands. For clarification, the engagement of specialists such as risk engineers is invaluable (Chapter 8.1). A further source for understanding natural peril exposures is the well-known mappings. This brings me to the issue of "underwriting curiosity" vs "natural hazard mapping".

Natural Hazard Mapping

When searching for "natural hazards mapping methods and techniques" via Google, there are, believe it or not, approximately 287 million results! This clearly underlines the interest in this specific topic, which we will explore further in this chapter.

In general, hazard maps provide detailed information about the causes, course, spatial scope, intensity and probability of occurrence of natural hazard events. Every insurance company uses the natural hazard mapping tool that has the best fit for its needs, whether it has been created internally or purchased from a pioneer in this field, such as Swiss Re (CatNet®) or Munich Re (NATHAN), which I used as my companion and great assistant for many years.

There is also the Geo Research Centre in Potsdam, which engages in the early detection of earthquakes, plus the Global Earthquake Model (GEM), which has the same purpose of assisting not only insurers but also governments and the public in risk assessment and mitigation. I have to apologise to all the other providers of natural hazard maps for not naming them here. There are of course many more valuable maps, but listing them would be beyond the scope of this book.

The most important questions for insurance companies concern how they can underwrite natural perils and what capital requirements should be combined with the set deployment of the underwriting capacity strategy. Relying solely on a single map in dealing with the uncertainties of natural perils will not be sufficient as such maps and studies cannot provide 100% security. Since 9/11, nothing is impossible.

In this context, an anecdote comes to mind, which I would like to share with you. When I started my international property underwriting career with the "Zurich" Group, I had the opportunity to attend the Munich Re Fire Course in Munich. The participants came from all over the world. Over the 2-week course, we were introduced to various aspects of sound underwriting by a number of specialists from Munich Re. One lecturer presented the definitions of natural perils. When he explained "hail" and later on "snow pressure", one of my participating colleagues from an insurance company in Kenya asked the question "what is the difference between hail and snow pressure?" I could hardly hold myself back from laughing because, for me, it was absolutely clear what the difference is. The lecturer professionally explained the difference to him and asked my Kenyan colleague whether the explanation was good enough for him to understand. He responded in clear words, "yes, I fully understand the difference. I shall go back to my country and include snow pressure in my local insurance policy for no money". At that point, nobody could restrain their laughter any more. How beautiful is this story! Some years ago, I came across an article in a newspaper, "'Snow' Falls in Kenya and Everyone Loses Their Minds" (www.okayafrica.com), which read as follows:

KENYA—Much to their surprise residents of Nyahururu, Kenya, woke up to snow on a morning. Many flocked to the streets, brandishing their cell phones to capture this odd occurrence, while others took to social media, to voice their disbelief. However, the Kenyan Meteorological Department was quick to point out that it wasn't snow, but rather, a particularly aggressive hail storm.

https://www.okayafrica.com

Nonetheless, some of the social media reactions to the strange weather were downright hilarious.

Remembering the story of my Kenyan colleague in Munich, I realised something very important: to be curious is not a given; it is a gift! With his curiosity, he was able to explore possibilities for including snow pressure in his local policy.

Uncertainties exist and always will; therefore, there is a need to combine natural hazard maps with a search for previous loss experience at the exposed sites, looking for tendencies and probabilities and keeping in mind climate change effects, extreme weather developments and so on.

4.1.3 All Risks

The Fact Is That "All Risks" Does Not Cover All Risks

In insurance terms, "all risks" means that the policy will cover all risks **except** those excluded under the policy. A policy that includes "all risks" is the type that most companies pay for to protect their assets and property financially, bearing in mind that an all-risk policy does not necessarily guarantee that the property will be covered against all forms of perils.

As described in Chapter 4.3.2 on onus of proof, the trigger for coverage under an "all risk" policy is physical loss or damage to property. An insured must prove that physical damage or loss has occurred before the burden of proof shifts to the insurer, who then has to prove that an exclusion applies to the coverage. For example, a small business that experienced a power outage may file a claim citing physical loss. The insurance company, on the other hand, might reject the claim, stating that the company experienced a loss of income from a mere loss of property use, which is not the same as a physical loss of property.

Let us look at an example, which shows that "all risks" does not cover all risks. Cases like the following often end up in courts for the legal interpretation of and ruling over an insurance policy's wording.

Does "All Risk" Property Insurance Cover Pandemics?

The question of whether an "all-risk" insurance policy should cover business losses resulting from the COVID-19 pandemic continues to dominate industry headlines, with a casino based in Miami, Florida, suing its insurer over a denied claim. The operators of Magic City Casino filed the lawsuit in the federal court in South Florida, as the *News Service of Florida* reported. The complaint named four insurance companies, which allegedly wrongfully denied the casino over business interruption losses.

The lawsuit claimed that the four companies had sold "all-risk" property insurance policies to the casino, which included coverage of business interruption losses. "The policies are all-risk", the lawsuit claimed. "In an all-risk insurance policy, all risks of loss are covered unless they are specifically excluded."

Magic City Casino also noted in its complaint that it was not suing other insurers that sold policies that specifically excluded coverage for things such as viruses. The lawsuit argued that the casino could not operate due to the shutdown orders issued by Governor Ron DeSantis and local officials. The disputed policies contain identical sections about providing coverage for losses resulting from an "order of civil or military authority", the complaint maintained.

"As a result of the presence of COVID-19 and the closure orders, plaintiff ... sustained a suspension of business operations, sustained losses of business income, and incurred extra expenses", the lawsuit stated. "Plaintiff has also sustained business income losses due to direct physical loss or physical damage at the premises of dependent properties." Magic City's lawsuit did not specify how much money the casino was seeking in the case.

The *News Service of Florida* said that none of the insurers had filed a response to the lawsuit.[9]

If you think that this is a single case ending up in a court for the legal interpretation of wording after the outbreak of a pandemic, think twice and refer to the many other cases on the Internet. As a professional property underwriter, you use your expertise and experience and apply good faith and full prudence in drafting and tailoring the wording, and you may even seek the advice of the legal as well as the actuarial department with the best knowledge; still, we cannot cover all human elements, such as perception and understanding, and therefore it is no surprise that, after all the professional work we have done, we end up in courts to justify our case, for example the pandemic, cyber-attack, 9/11 – the list is not exhaustive!

The Conclusion Is: "All Risks" Does Not Cover All Risks

How Will a Property Insurance Policy Respond to the Following Arising Risks?

- Industry 4.0/Internet of Things (IoT)
- Automated mobility
- New cyber risks
- Robotics
- Nano technology: dealing with or using "engineered nanoparticles"
- Additive manufacturing (3D printing)
- Construction materials
- Counterfeit products
- Electromagnetic fields/electromagnetic interference (EMF/EMI)
- Water and food scarcity
- Genetically modified organisms (GMOs)
- Endocrine disruptors

The captioned list is not comprehensive and may well evolve continuously over time.

Dealing with emerging risks is a challenge, especially for underwriters, in view of the rapidly changing legal, social and technological environment. Clairvoyancy skills are often required to be able to recognise negative developments at an early stage. A future-oriented coping strategy is therefore necessary to be able to react appropriately and promptly to specific threat situations. This concept should include elements such as the early detection and recording of emerging risks, analysis and the implementation of (underwriting) measures because risks contain not only challenges but also opportunities that need to be exploited and may also lead to a competitive advantage as a first mover.

What we regard today as a given, something that is absolutely normal and makes common sense, was once perceived as impossible, not to say futuristic, adventurous and almost science fiction. Do you remember your first computer (PC)? How would Leonardo da Vinci (1452–1519), as an underwriter, feel, looking back, about Apple? Apple-1 was designed in 1976 by Steve Wozniak, a native of Sunnyvale, California, and marketed by his friend, Steve Jobs, and it was a single-board computer for hobbyists. With an order in hand for 50 assembled systems from The Byte Shop, a computer store in Mountain View, California, the pair started a new company, naming it Apple Computer, Inc. In all, about 200 of the boards were sold before Apple announced the follow-up Apple II a year later as a ready-to-use computer for consumers, a model that sold in the millions for nearly two decades.[10]

In the 1970s, the world was ecstatic about the evolution of consumers' usable computers. The focus was not only on the further developments, novelty and innovations but primarily on how to obtain one of this magic machines! Why would someone think about the possible risks of such an endurable possession when the focus was on satisfying one's need to take part in the evolution and be part of the epoch? I do not think that, at that time, anybody was questioning any possible future risks that could make our lives in some ways more difficult – Y2K and cyber risk.

News such as hackers having stolen cryptocurrency to the amount of USD600 million overnight seemed impossible when personal computers were introduced. Unfortunately, it is a fact and almost a standard procedure today to which we are becoming accustomed.

This again implies the importance in underwriting of looking ahead and not only at past experiences of losses, claims and models established on past events and available data. Identifying new risks arising from the above list and preparing to deal with them are a continuous process. Many of these risks do not belong to a property policy at first glance now, but might they suddenly have an immense impact in the near future? If not, then you need to develop your underwriting position regarding why they do not belong to property (e.g., infectious diseases and cyber-attacks in the past) and be prepared to defend this position in the courts. You probably agree with me about the dilemma of acting vs reacting – do not "wait for the problem to knock at your door" but act now as this is a much better position and differentiates one from the crowd.

As mentioned earlier, expect the unexpected to happen!

4.2 Business Interruption (BI) Section

Claudio Böttcher

4.2.1 Broad-Spectrum Considerations

As a short introduction to this topic, let us remind ourselves of a couple of key aspects of business interruption insurance:

- Business interruption (BI) insurance covers losses following an insured incident interrupting or interfering with the business of the policyholder.
- The fundamental requirement when tailoring business interruption cover to customer needs is to understand the nature of business interruption coverage and the way in which a particular business operates. We can hence tailor the cover to a customer's activity by using either the gross profit and gross revenue form (as for service providers such as hotels, accountants, etc.) or the gross rental form (as for property developers) for those markets that follow the UK methodology. Alternatively, a gross earnings or business income coverage form is available in those markets that follow the US methodology.
- In general, if there is a separate BI policy, this will cover the same perils as the material damage (property) policy. In addition, it will be subject to the so-called material damage proviso. This warranty will require a material damage policy to be in place to enable the warranties of the material damage policy to have an effect on the BI policy as well and to ensure that the funds for reinstatement or repair are available. The material damage proviso is typically not included in the US policy forms since normally BI is insured as an extension to the property policy.

- Turnover is the income of the business derived from the sale and delivery of goods and services. We use turnover to measure the effects of damage on the business. Turnover figures are readily available on a regular basis and reflect seasonal influences as well as the trend of the business. In simple terms, the turnover of a business is allocated within a business as follows:

  - Variable costs: these decrease directly with any reduction in turnover. There is no need to be insured. Examples are purchases (less discounts) of raw materials, carriage, packaging and freight (other than the insured's own transportation).
  - Overhead expenses (also called fixed costs): these do not vary directly with the changes in turnover and are hence insurable. Examples are electricity, gas, water, telecommunications and many others.
  - Net profit (or loss): this is the result after the deduction of the variable costs and overhead expenses from the turnover.

- In the jargon of the business interruption policy (UK gross profit or gross revenue difference basis), we use the following terms:

  - *Uninsured working expenses*: these are variable costs that are not insured and that will be listed within the BI specification's wording.
  - *Standing charges*: these are the overhead expenses and should be insured.
  - *Net profit*: this is the net profit or loss, as described above.
  - *The gross profit* is either

    - The sum of the insured standing charges and net profit (the addition basis seldom being used these days) or
    - The turnover less uninsured working expenses (the difference basis, which is the most commonly used form of the loss of profit BI wording used in the UK and in many countries around the world).

  - *Indemnity period*: the period beginning with the occurrence of the incident and ending not later than the maximum period thereafter during which the results of the business are affected as a consequence.

- *Maximum indemnity period:* this states the number of months as agreed with the customer.

- A key aspect for you to remember when discussing insurance with your customer is the fact that the definition of gross profit in the BI policy may differ from that used in the accounting practice. This is particularly the case for manufacturing risks and is due to the fact that accountants are very often trying to determine the accurate cost of the goods to be sold. As a result, when establishing the accounting gross profit, accountants may already have considered the deduction from the turnover of direct materials, direct labour and factory overheads to arrive at such an amount.[11] If we consider, for example, the insurable gross profit as usually defined on a standard different basis policy form:

Turnover plus closing stock and work in progress

Less

Uninsured working expenses plus opening stock and work in progress.

The insurable gross profit may differ from the trading gross profit as established by the accountants. Therefore, the uninsured working expenses should only be those expenditures that vary in direct proportion to the turnover. It is very important that you understand this difference and that you are in a position to explain the difference to your customers. This point has created considerable confusion for customers; hence, many insurance companies and market organisations have developed so-called business interruption cover calculators to help customers to obtain the right gross profit sum insured.

There is nothing more awkward than upsetting customers following an under-insured loss event resulting from a misunderstanding in the sum's insured calculation. Understanding the difference between insurable gross profit and accountants' gross profit is therefore one of an underwriter's duties.

- International business interruption insurance: There are a number of differences in the coverage as it is provided locally. The most notable difference is between the approach of the UK and that of the US. If you would like to learn about these differences in much more detail, we recommend reading Chapter 12 of *Riley on Business Interruption Insurance* (9th Edition) by Harry Roberts. This book is a great resource for anyone who wants to learn about business interruption insurance in detail and is probably the best one that I have read so far.

  Why is this important for you to know? It is essential when setting up an international property insurance programme that there is clarity about which methodology will be applicable in the case of a claim affecting the master policy. It is not only the US that uses these forms; other countries also follow the US methodology.

  In the praxis, insurance companies may provide a master policy in which both the UK and the US forms are applicable. Often, the customer may have the condition to choose which form will be applicable to the relevant loss. We have also seen some forms in which both coverages are included but it is stated that gross profit is applicable to losses to insured premises outside the USA only and gross earnings are applicable to insured premises in the USA only. To avoid disputes, it is necessary to state the applicable approach clearly in the policy wording. This is another key point relating to contract certainty, as explained more explicitly in section 4.3 on policy wordings.

4.2.2. Factors Affecting Business Interruption Underwriting Assessment

General Factors

The following basic checklist is the result of combining some of our technical reading with our personal underwriting experience and, very importantly, consultation with one of the key underwriting supporting pillars: risk engineering. The list is dynamic and not all-inclusive. You may want to expand it to include additional aspects based on your own experience and knowledge.

The following factors are relevant not only for underwriters but also for customers and brokers. If the customers' own exposures are not understood, the question that follows is "how can underwriters advise them on coverage, risk reduction and mitigation as well as aspects of contingency planning?"

Factors	Example of high-level issues/questions	Comments
Production arrangements	• Impact of loss on gross profit • Separation/protection of process/profit units: are there parallel lines or duplicate/alternative capacity?	Relevant for scenario modelling
Process controls and computers	• Reliance on automated process controls • Distributed control systems (commonly located on premises that are vulnerable and/or concentrated)	The year 2000 event (Y2K) did not materialise, but it alerted everyone to the modern dependence on system controls and data storage and protection. Some of the recent cyber-attacks highlight the issues around process control and computers:[12] • Capitol One breach • Weather Channel ransomware • US customs and border protection/ Perceptics • Citrix breach • Texas ransomware attacks • WannaCry • NotPetya • Ethereum

Bottleneck duplication	• Critical processing units • Access/material flow constraints • Storage or transport arrangements	Any available hazard analysis critical control point (HACCP) can help to determine where the critical point is.
Process support	• Critical tooling • Process moulds • Technical drawings • Quality of records/samples • Critical spares/consumable items	What is the ability to recreate duplicates, plans and specifications?
Utilities	• Power generation/ transmission • Compressed air/gases • Steam • Process/building heating/ cooling • Water supply/treatment • Blowers • Pollution control equipment	All utilities should be considered separately. What, for example, is the effect of telecom failure on a sales operation dependent on an offshore call centre?
Restoration of buildings and machinery	• Purpose-built facilities • Location-specific facilities • Long lead time equipment	Heavy manufacturing, electronics, pharmaceuticals, etc. Mining, infrastructure, retail, accommodation, etc. Imported machinery, one-off designs, transformers, etc. We have to pay attention here to the maximum indemnity periods and the availability of restoration specialists.

Restoration of finished stock	• Long production periods • High inventory levels	E.g., shipbuilding New product launch, seasonal markets (demand or production)
Seasonal fluctuation	• Seasonal demand	Holiday stock (Christmas time) Weather (snow skis) Travel and accommodation
Seasonal supply	• Crops • Weather constraints • Regulatory constraints	
Spare capacity – within the site/operation	• Multiple production lines • Spare shift capacity • Ability to utilise capacity	Cross compatibility, changeover time/ parts, skilled labour availability Storage/delivery constraints, labour constraints, regulatory constraints
Spare capacity – external	• Generic products or components • Compatible operations • Co-operative competitors	Market assistance following a loss might be seen as out of time, but we believe it is still worth verifying whether this is possible.
Market	• Position/consequences: · High market share · Strong brand position · Strong competitors · Low barriers to entry · High changeover costs for customers	Is there enhanced vulnerability?

Spare capacity – within the group	• Sister plants with spare capacity:
	  ◦ Transport constraints and costs
	  ◦ Product and equipment compatibility
	  ◦ Packaging/labelling differences
	  ◦ Regulatory/market constraints
	• Alternative facilities nearby, e.g., hotel chains	

Just in time	• Increased vulnerability • Low or no inventory • Enhanced contingent business interruption (CBI): reliance on suppliers	A critical aspect to consider; for example, one customer had raw materials delivered every 4 hours.

Customer dependencies	• Single or few major customers
	  ◦ Retailers
	  ◦ Distributors
	  ◦ Industrial customers
	• Distribution chain
	  ◦ Hotel chains
	  ◦ Booking systems/ computers
	  ◦ Internet hosting	

External supplier dependencies	• Raw materials
	  ◦ Primary producers
	  ◦ Storage
	  ◦ Transport
	• Sub-components
	  ◦ Manufacturers
	  ◦ Inventory
	  ◦ Transport
		Some industries are now so horizontally and vertically integrated that a loss anywhere in the world will have a global impact.
		The 2011 Thailand flood and 2011 Japan earthquake are some examples.

External utility dependencies	• Power • Gas • Water • Sewers • Other utilities	An explosion at a gas plant in East Gippsland, Australia: after Victoria's gas operator declared a Level 5 emergency, the plant was completely shut down and the flow of gas stopped. The supply was offline for 12 days. A total of 98% of Victoria's gas was supplied by the affected fields. 1.4 million domestic, commercial and industrial customers were affected, including the chemical, metal manufacturing and brewing industries. The loss of sales reached approximately AUD1.3 billion. Note: The above example highlights efficiencies and sensitivities. For some industries, utility downtimes can have a severe business interruption impact.

Internal dependencies	• Increasing specialisation:
	  • Specialised plants – components, tooling
	  • Centralised services –design, information systems, business services, laboratories/testing
	  • Consolidation of warehousing and transport	

Denial of access	• Site-specific, such as neighbouring properties, e.g., chemical plants, or politically sensitive sites
	• Locality-specific catastrophic perils – flood, severe weather, etc.
	• Infrastructure
	  ◦ Road
	  ◦ Rail
	  ◦ Ports	

Business continuity planning (BCP)	• BCP is the major business interruption control after asset protection. BCP is intended not to prevent disruptions but to help a company to survive should a disruption occur • The quality and application of BCP vary massively • Many people confuse an IT disaster recovery plan (DRP) with BCP	We believe that BCP is probably one of the most important factors in business interruption underwriting risk assessment today. The point is that, if an insured company is not ready for a potential interruption, it may not recover fully or at all. Question: How many companies had considered the pandemic outbreak of COVID-19 in their potential interruption scenarios and, if so, what were the measures included to reduce or mitigate such an interruption loss? Underwriters are strongly advised to consult their risk engineering department.

In addition to the above, the following factors are explored in much more detail.

4.2.3 Potential Business Interruption Loss

Over the last few years, the cost of business interruption losses has been constantly increasing. On average, these losses are roughly 30% to 50% higher than the property damage loss.[13] For certain industries, the potential BI component of the overall PD/BI loss can be as high as 90% (e.g., in the mining industry). In an attempt to become more profitable, many industries have modified their production strategies, leading to a number of reductions in previously existing redundancies and in many cases even a lack of alternatives should an event occur. The cause of the loss is triggered not only by fire or explosions but also by increased occurrences of other causes, such as disasters due to hazardous (geological, geophysical or hydrometeorological) events, machinery breakdown, cyber risk and others.

Notably, arrangements to improve production costs, such as just-in-time or lean manufacturing, have made supply chains less resilient. For example, a loss at one production site in one country could have a significant impact on a production site in another country. We will elaborate in section 4.2.11 on supply chain resilience. At this point, it is crucial for you as an underwriter to understand the potential implications and exposures given the activity of the customer you are about to underwrite. By working with your risk engineers, you should be in a better position to understand, based on their established key exposure scenarios, what a loss could look like and what the potential BI component could be. Remember that very often a small property damage loss can trigger a massive BI loss. For example, small pressing machine damage of USD400K triggered a CBI loss of USD45 million. The affected single-source supplier delivered a unique component to a car manufacturing company.

The following example should also help you to visualise the potential size of the BI component following a property damage loss:

> Massive landslide at Utah copper mine
>
> On the evening of 10 April 2013, a massive landslide occurred at the Bingham Canyon copper mine near Salt Lake City, Utah, USA. … In total, roughly 65 million cubic meters of material was deposited, making the cumulative event likely the largest non-volcanic landslide to have occurred in North America in modern times.[14]

At that time, it was said that the loss could cost underwriters between USD700 million and USD1 billion. We are not aware of the value of the final settlement, but this loss gives you an idea of the proportions of such an event. While there was some damage to equipment and to a building structure in the mine, given the fact that this is an open pit, we believe that the BI loss was notably the greater component of the overall loss.

In another example, a nickel–copper mine in Spain resumed its operation almost 2 years after heavy rains caused a slide at this plant. Can you imagine the size of the BI loss?

> Fire following flood at refinery in La Plata, Argentina.
>
> It is said that between April 2 and April 3, 2013 the rainfall was greater than 400mm within a period of 4 hours. The area affected by the severe storm included the city of La Plata (the capital of Buenos Aires province) and the conglomerate of Buenos Aires. It would appear that roughly 90% of the city of La Plata was flooded.

I remember at the time of the event that underwriters and other related insurance industry people were arguing that the area is not a typical flood-prone area. Following our underwriting curiosity, we carried out quick search on the Internet, which revealed a report from 2005:[15]

> Over the last two decades of the 20th Century, important floods in Del Plata Basin have been caused by the global climate change. Greater La Plata (comprising La Plata city and the towns of Berisso and Ensenada) is not exempt from this problem …
>
> Floods at Greater La Plata are the result of the confluence of three factors: precipitation (mainly when high rain fails), groundwater tables (whose upward pressure has increased due to their elevation and the south east wind (which makes the river rise).

Following the 2013 event, the engineering faculty of the University of La Plata produced a report detailing a long list of some of the causes of such flooding. It included not only the magnitude of the storm and its extraordinary characteristics but also the lack of an overarching risk management approach to flooding in the whole affected area. It was quite detailed and is worth reading.

As a result of this flash flood during heavy rain, a fire broke out in a refinery located in the area. The fire directly affected a coke unit and a distillation unit, causing the shutdown of the entire refinery. The rain overwhelmed the storm drainage system, resulting in hydrocarbons being washed out of the drains and around the site. The furnaces had been shut down but were still hot enough to ignite the hydrocarbons, resulting in this fire following the flood.

The amount of the loss was estimated at between USD500 million and USD800 million (depending on which report you read[16,17]). We believe that roughly 80% to 90% is the portion of the business interruption loss and 10% to 20% is the material damage component. We have included this loss in the business interruption perspective given our explanations at the beginning of this section, but you can also consider it within the context of section 4.1.2 on natural perils. In our view, we can consider it from both perspectives.

"It is quite an unusual event" was one of the first comments that we heard at the time. We believe, though, that more events of this nature will occur given the current extreme weather trends. As confirmed by our empirical observations over the last 20 years, flash floods are no longer extraordinary events.

Beyond the tools that you may have available, such as maps or models, we believe that searching for local information about previous occurrences is an underwriting duty that is as important as the use of all the available tools. Last but not least, always expect the unexpected to happen. In this case, the industry did not expect this flood to happen; as we know, it did.

How many losses do you know of that were unexpected ones? The questions for us underwriters are how likely it is that an unlikely event (or one believed to be unlikely) will happen and if so what the financial implications are.

Every year, various insurance/reinsurance companies as well as broking houses produce a number of reports. We urge you to spend some time reading these reports as they provide invaluable information relating to underwriting and claims trends. As part of our underwriting curiosity, it is vital to keep up to date with market trends, not only at the local level but also globally. In today's interconnected world, we cannot dismiss the impact of these trends on our daily underwriting work.

Finally, take time to learn from individual losses in your own company as well as market losses. More often than not, these losses are a great source of underwriting knowledge and a further basis for your continuous development programme.

4.2.4 Interdependency

Large companies may need to cover the reciprocal dependency within the group. This is relevant when different sites are dependent on each other given the exchange of goods; for example, one site produces a material or component that is then used by another site in the manufacturing of goods. The coverage is then provided through an extension clause called interdependency, which is normally included in the master policy only. The selected limit should reflect the exposure to an interdependency loss.

In general, the clause will state that any loss arising from business interruption at the insured premises as a result of loss or damage to the property insured having occurred at another insured premises will be covered. Understanding the exposure and its financial implications is essential before selecting the limit for this extension. Given the complex supply chain structure that many companies have, you would be well advised to consult your risk engineering department to gain a better overview of what you can expect in the case of a loss.

You need to consider the interdependency loss scenario in addition to your overall loss scenario calculation, like other extensions (e.g., debris removal, professional fees, etc.) that come in addition to the basic driving peril (fire, explosion or other peril) loss estimate calculated by your risk engineer. This will be the basis (after you are satisfied, following your risk assessment, that the risk is within your corporate risk appetite, quality and sustainable pricing strategy and underwriting policy) on which you will deploy your capacity.

Interdependency exposures are very often not well analysed by underwriters and sometimes even disregarded, but again, given the supply chain complexities these days, it is important to pay more attention to them and avoid surprises should a loss occur. It might be difficult for some customers even to provide relevant information to assess their exposure. If this is the case, it will show the weakness on the customers' side in understanding their own exposure. We recall the case of an aircraft manufacturer that was not able to provide a split of the business interruption sum insured by location globally. Can you imagine the consequences – the time involved in settling the claim and the potential discussions if an agreement could not be found with the customer – if a loss occurred? How much would you have written from such an unknown exposure, if anything?

In a few cases, customers require an interdependency extension to be included in each and every local policy. Our view is to refuse this type of request for the customers' own benefit. In such a scenario, the complexity of settling a claim would be enormous and probably subject to disputes. On the insurance company side, such a request would make it extremely difficult to allow for a proper exposure assessment and to handle accumulation exposures. Last but not least, how would such an exposure be priced?

4.2.5 Contingent Business Interruption (CBI)

Definition

CBI is actually the American denomination for what in the UK used to be called "property away from the insured premises". The language of the CBI extension will depend on whether the policy is a US-based (gross earnings or business income coverage form) or UK-based (gross profit, gross rentals or gross revenue) methodology, but, in essence, CBI will cover the loss of income of your customer in the event that a supplier or customer experiences a physical loss resulting in interference or disruption of your customer's own business.

Basic Categories of CBI Extensions

On the condition that the loss must result directly from the interruption of your insured's business and as a consequence of a physical loss of or damage to the property covered under the property damage and business interruption policy caused by an insured peril, the main categories are the following:

- Specified supplier (*)
- Specified customer
- Direct unspecified supplier (*)
- Direct unspecified customer

(*) Note that these extensions do not include the interruption of or interference with the business as a result of any interruption of electricity, gas, water or telecommunication supplies. There is a specific extension for utility suppliers.

Other Common CBI Extensions

To supplement the basic categories, there are a number of additional CBI extensions. Below, we highlight those that require particular underwriting attention.

4.2.6 Utilities (Formerly Called Public Utilities (UK Form) or Off-Premises Services (US Form)

Under this extension, coverage will be provided to the business interruption of your insured due to the failure of the supply of electricity, gas, water or telecommunication services.

4.2.7 Prevention of or Hindrance to Access (UK) or Ingress/Egress (US)

Coverage will be provided for the business interruption of your insured following "loss or destruction of or damage to property in the vicinity which shall prevent or hinder the use of the premises or access thereto, whether the premises or property of the insured therein shall be damaged or not". [18]

4.2.8 Loss of Attraction (UK)/Attraction Properties (US)

Coverage will be provided for the business interruption of your insured following "loss in consequence of damage to property in the vicinity of the premises which causes a fall in the number of customers attracted to the vicinity of the premises whether the property used by the insured for the purpose of the business shall be damaged or not".[19]

4.2.9 Notifiable Disease, Vermin, Defective Sanitary Arrangements, Murder and Suicide (UK)

The following is the standard wording of the Association of British Insurers (ABI) for this extension. There are different versions depending on the activity involved:

- Hotels, Restaurants and Public Houses
- Schools, Private Hospitals, etc.
- Food Processors and Distributors

For illustration purposes, we quote the Hotels, Restaurant and Public Houses version in full as it will help to guide you to the relevant aspects to consider under the risk assessment section below:

> The insurance… shall… extend to include loss resulting from interruption or interference with the Business carried on by the Insured at the Premises in consequence of:

1 (a) any occurrence of a Notifiable Disease (as defined below) at the Premises or attributable to food or drink supplied from the Premises

(b) any discovery of an organism at the Premises likely to result in the occurrence of a Notifiable Disease

(c) any occurrence of a Notifiable Disease (in the town/borough of…) (within a radius of 25 miles of the Premises

2 the discovery of vermin or pests at the Premises which causes restrictions on the use of the Premises on the order or advice of the competent local authority

3 any accident causing the defects in the drains or other sanitary arrangements at the Premises which causes restrictions on the use of the Premises on the order of a competent local authority

4 any occurrence of murder or suicide at the Premises

Special Conditions

1 Notifiable Disease shall mean illness sustained by any person resulting from

Food or drink poisoning, or

(a) Any human infectious or human contagious disease (excluding
(b) Acquired Immune Deficiency Syndrome (AIDS), an outbreak of which the competent local authority has stipulated shall be notified to them

2 For the purpose of this memorandum

Indemnity Period shall mean the period during which the results of the Business shall be affected in consequence of the occurrence, discovery or accident, beginning

(a) In the case of 1 and 4 above, with the date of the occurrence or discovery

(b) In the case of 2 and 3 above, with the date from which the restriction on the Premises are applied and ending not later than the Maximum Indemnity Period thereafter.

Maximum Indemnity Period shall mean……months

Premises shall mean only those locations stated in the Premises definition; in the event that the policy includes an extension which deems loss destruction or damage at other locations to be an Incident such extension shall not apply to this memorandum.

3 The Insurer shall not be liable under this memorandum for any costs incurred in the cleaning, repair, replacement, recall or checking of property.

4 The Insurer shall only be liable for the loss arising at those Premises which are directly affected by the occurrence discovery or accident.

Notably, over the years, the market has developed innumerable different versions of this extension, ranging from the above to very wild and extremely broad versions covering any infectious disease, with no distance limitation (beyond 25 miles or the vicinity to anywhere) and no limited indemnity period, including physical costs and many other inefficiencies that question the underwriting intent as well as the results of a claim settlement.

As we speak, COVID-19 is exerting an impact on society globally, and many discussions are taking place as to whether the resulting losses are covered, not only in regard to "infectious disease" extensions but also concerning "closure by a competent authority". Note that, while infectious disease generally covers the discovery of a disease at and/or within 25 miles/vicinity of the insured premises, the closure by a competent authority will respond to losses due to the hindrance in accessing the insured premises because it has been closed on the order of the relevant authority, for example the police or the government, as it has been the case with COVID-19.

As mentioned above, one of the challenges is that there are so many variations of these extensions in the market that it is practically impossible to make a general statement regarding whether these extensions will or can respond to all or most of the COVID-19-related business interruption losses. At this point, it is probably better to reflect and review what the insurance industry can learn and how it can perform better in the future, keeping in mind first and foremost our customers.

The following are some of these reflections:

- We do not believe that, when these extensions were crafted, for instance in the UK in the 1930s, that the underwriting intent was to provide for such a massive pandemic risk accumulation as is the case with COVID-19 losses. Many underwriters have naively thought that this is just a nice extension to the basic policy providing added value for the customer: a valid and honest intention but one that probably failed to consider all the possible implications.

- At the time when these extensions were developed, the world was not as interconnected and globalised as it is now. Disease outbreaks were probably more local and/or regional in effect than they are today (e.g., SARS in 2003 in Hong Kong).
- We should always bear in mind that it is not only the "what" question that is relevant in underwriting. The question of "how we want to do things" is probably even more pertinent. A good colleague stated, "we underwrite what we know and we know what we underwrite": a very basic but extremely important principle in all that we do, which leads to the question: have we really applied it when we underwrote these extensions? Have we thought about the worst pandemic scenarios in our assessment and the potential accumulation exposure? Have we priced for it? Was this our underwriting intention? Have we properly managed our customer's expectations?

Time will show the result of our final conclusions and what we can improve for us as underwriters and for our customers, but it should serve as an underwriting lesson for the future when we consider questions of what and how.

4.2.10 Contingent Business Interruption (CBI) Risk Assessment

Over time, the underwriting praxis in dealing with CBI exposures has changed substantially. The factors affecting this change are mainly due to the supply chain transformation evidenced in most industries through globalisation. Many industries have also changed their business model, for example from the full production of a product to an assembling approach. You can research how the automotive and electronics industries, as examples, have evolved during the last 40 years.

The common praxis in the 1980s was to provide a sub-limit by supplier, which was very often expressed as a percentage of the customer's turnover. Today, it is common to receive a list of thousands of suppliers with the expectation that all of them will be covered under a single sub-limit. In addition, you may receive a request to include a lower but still substantial sub-limit for direct unnamed suppliers or customers and not least to include extensions to suppliers of suppliers, also called tier 2 or tier 3 suppliers.

What are the key elements of your risk assessment (in addition or complementary to those mentioned in section 4.2.2 and for what purpose?

Specified supplier	Evaluation
Name of supplier	It is not uncommon for an insurance company that the same supplier is also insured under another policyholder's insurance PD/BI policy including a CBI extension; or this supplier is insured as a direct insured by your company. The name of the supplier together with the address will allow you to consult your records for accumulation purposes. Remember that CBI can trigger substantial accumulations due to the same event.
Address	For the same reasons as above. We have seen information being provided on, for example, a PowerPoint slide indicating only the logo of the supplier and no indication of which location is meant to be included. This very limited information will not allow you to identify any accumulation or to determine whether a supplier's premises are, for instance, located in a disaster-prone area.
Are critical products or services delivered?	Determine the criticality of the supplier based on the following features: • Single source supplier (*) – "the sourcing of a particular supplier is purposefully chosen by the buying organisation, even, when other suppliers are available". • Sole source supplier (*) – "sourcing takes place when only one supplier for the required item is available". • Non-critical supplier – sourcing of relevant items that are available widely from different suppliers. (*)[20] This information is relevant to underwriting, particularly if your risk engineer is involved in determining the potential loss that you can expect.

Accumulation potential	Check your records about potential accumulations. Remember that it is highly possible that your organisation is insuring a critical supplier either directly or indirectly via CBI cover. A physical loss at a critical supplier insured within your organisation cannot only result in significant direct property damage and business interruption but also in a swarm of CBI associated losses. See a potential example below.
Business continuity planning (BCP)	As mentioned in sections 4.2.2 and 8.3, business continuity planning (BCP) is the major business interruption control after asset protection, in particular for managing supply chain risk disruptions. Particular attention should be paid to whether the BCP handles disruptions from critical suppliers. Note that, according to the Business Continuity Institute (BCI), companies that currently employ BCP as an integral part of their procurement and supplier selection process are in the minority. Hence, it is very importa nt to include a key element in your CBI assessment.
Insured perils	The underwriting policy of your organisation may impose restrictions on CBI coverage for a number of perils, such as natural perils, terrorism and so on. Irrespective of your underwriting policy, it is important to understand the potential implications when it comes to disaster events of natural hazards such as earthquakes, windstorms, floods and so on and the probability of unknown accumulation exposures, for example the 2011 in floods Thailand and earthquake in Japan affecting suppliers of key industries, such as the automotive and electronic industries.

Accumulation Example

The insurance company Beta provides insurance to its different customers through different policies as follows:

Line-setting consideration for the insurance company Beta	Amount USD million
Company Alpha – Direct property damage and business interruption. The activity is the manufacturing of car components for the automotive industry. The policy covers damage to the company's own property due to a number of perils, such as fire. The risk engineering established the loss expectancy for the location with a major loss scenario as USD300 million.	300
Company Auto One – The business interruption section includes CBI coverage. The company is a car manufacturer. Among the named critical suppliers, Company Alpha is listed with a sub-limit of USD100 million. The risk engineer could not determine the potential loss scenario and amount; hence, for the purpose of your line setting, the full amount has to be considered.	100
Company Auto Two – The business interruption section includes CBI coverage. The company is a car manufacturer. Among the named critical suppliers, Company Alpha is listed with a sub-limit of USD100 million. The risk engineer could determine the potential loss scenario at USD50 million.	50
Company Auto Three – The business interruption section includes CBI coverage. The company is a car manufacturer. Among the named critical suppliers, Company Alpha is listed with a sub-limit of USD100 million. The risk engineer could not determine the potential loss scenario; hence, for the purpose of your line setting, the full amount has to be considered.	100
Total loss amount that you can expect in the case of a fire or any other peril constituting the governing peril at the premises of Company Alpha following an insured peril.	**550**

Cases like that described above are not rare or uncommon these days. CBI accumulation is one of the greatest challenges that many insurance companies face for all the reasons already described elsewhere in this book. As underwriters, it is critical that we are able to identify such loss potential scenarios to determine properly how much capacity we can put at risk and to avoid overcommitting our company and hence jeopardising the profitability of the book of business.

In addition, accumulation management is relevant to reinsurance recoveries should a loss event occur. In general, the practice is that, for multiple insureds with common suppliers and/or customers for which the CBI accumulation is known, each insured will be considered as one risk unless, at the time when the risk is accepted by the insurance company, the line setting has been established based on the accumulation of the location with the largest loss potential exposure including the associated CBI element. If the latter is not the case, then there is a high probability that each insured will be considered as one risk.

Specified customer	Evaluation
Name of customer	Similar considerations as for specified named suppliers. A manufacturing company must face the situation that a customer is not able to accept the delivery of a product due to an incident at the customer's premises. This is relevant when the company is delivering to a limited number of customers. Note that this extension refers to those cases in which the insured is delivering products or services to a customer through a contracted or trading relationship.
Address	Same considerations as for specified named suppliers.
Are critical products or services delivered?	Same considerations as for specified named suppliers.
Accumulation potential	Same considerations as for specified named suppliers.
Business continuity planning (BCP)	Same considerations as for specified named suppliers.
Insured perils	Same considerations as for specified named suppliers.

Direct unnamed supplier or customer	Evaluation
Insured's request to include this extension	More often than not, your insured will make this request because of the uncertainty regarding whether all suppliers and/or customers have been included in the specified named list. Insurance companies will in general accept the inclusion of this extension but may want to exclude certain perils of, for example, nature, terrorism and so on due to the unknown exposure and potential unintended accumulation. Some insurance companies may also want to avoid an unnamed basis for tier 3 or tier 4 (suppliers of suppliers or customers of customers) as it becomes unmanageable to determine any potential exposure. Accumulation is basically impossible under such conditions.

Notifiable disease, vermin, defective sanitary arrangements, murder and suicide (UK)	Evaluation
Notifiable disease	Are only notifiable diseases covered or any sort of disease? Are they named in the policy extension and is a definition included? Which are excluded? Note: Some policies exclude any infectious diseases that have been declared as a pandemic by the World Health Organisation (see important additional notes below).

Distance limitation	At its origin, this was limited to 25 miles from the insured premises. The creativity of some underwriters has resulted in it being amended or replaced with terms such as "within the vicinity". Note that, in many jurisdictions, the term vicinity has no legal definition and hence might lead to potential disputes in the case of a loss. Consider where the insured premises are located. If you provide this extension in a policy covering risks in, for example, Hong Kong, the 25-mile distance will probably include mainland China as well. If the insured premises are located in Basel, Switzerland, the 25 miles will extend to Germany and France as well. Remember to identify your underwriting intent and never follow a cut-and-paste approach even if the insurance intermediary asks for it unless you are able to assess the risk and alignment with your company's risk appetite and underwriting policy.
Maximum indemnity period	Consider a maximum indemnity period commensurate with the exposure. Typically, these are lower than the general ones in the business interruption section.
Costs incurred in the cleaning, repair, replacement, recall or checking of property	The ABI version quoted earlier in this section explicitly excludes this type of costs. If you still want to include them, then you would be well advised to consider the potential loss cost and embed it into your pricing considerations as these extra costs are very expensive.

Note related to COVID-19 pandemic-related losses:

At the time of writing this book, many American courts have ruled against coverage for business interruption loss due to COVID-19. In the UK, on 15 September 2020, the High Court decided, based on the sample of policy wordings presented by the Financial Conduct Authority (FCA), that most, but not all, of the disease clauses provided cover for losses connected to COVID-19. It also concluded that certain denial of access clauses provided cover, depending on the specific wording of how the business was affected by government measures, such as mandatory closure orders. The test case also clarified that the COVID-19 pandemic and the government and public response were a single cause of the covered loss, which is a key requirement for claims to be paid even if the policy provides cover. It is notable that the wordings represented by some insurers in the FCA test case reportedly did not provide cover for business interruption in relation to the COVID-19 outbreak.

On 15 January 2021, insurers were urged to pay up without delay after the judges of the Supreme Court dismissed the industry's arguments over the disputed claims. The insurance industry is expected to pay out over GBP1.8 billion in COVID-19-related claims across a range of products, including business interruption policies. Full details of the business interruption test case's court judgement can be found at www.fca.org.uk. We strongly recommend reading it. There are many lessons that the insurance industry can learn from this test case, relating in particular to proper policy crafting (underwriting intent) and contract certainty. Both are important not only from a wording clarity perspective but also from a customer trust point of view.

Finally, the Chartered Insurance Institute (CII) has urged insurance professionals to act now to avoid the need for legal proceedings like this FCA test case in the future. The organisation has urged the profession to focus on product governance processes, improving advice processes and establishing an approach to pandemics and other systemic risks that clearly establishes the scope of government intervention.

What has been the impact on property damage and business interruption losses resulting from COVID-19 in your country?

4.2.11 Supply Chain Resilience

As we have already discussed, supply chains have increased in terms of complexity and global interconnection. As a result, the consequences of disruptions are nowadays increasingly difficult to assess. The sources of potential disruptions are not limited but rather extremely wide as they can originate from innumerable causes. These can range from unknown exposures in the supply chain to disasters (natural or manmade hazards) and many others that do not necessarily stem from physical damage but that are also outside the company's control. Some examples are regulatory environment changes, the financial insolvency of a supplier, unplanned IT or telecommunication outage and loss of talent/skills.

A single disruption in the supply chain can not only have substantial financial implications but also damage the reputation of the company. Note the financial implications resulting from the 2011 Thailand flood (computer manufacturers were affected since 45% of the world's computer hard drive suppliers are located in the flooded area) or the 2011 Japan earthquake affecting the semiconductor and automotive industries. Further examples include the 2018 fire at a magnesium die-cast plant in the US, which disrupted the automotive supply chain globally; the explosion at a supplier site in Germany that produced Nylon 12 used for fluidic tight capacity plastic elements and fuel tank and pump functional modules in the automotive industry; and, last but not least, a fire at a Japanese supplier that produced P-valves for the braking system functional module. The Silicon Sea Belt in Asia is a further example of high supply chain concentration. Roughly 50% of the global semiconductor industry is concentrated in a geographic area involving countries such as Japan, Singapore, China, Taiwan and South Korea.

As explained in section 4.3.2, many industries have modified their production strategies, leading to a number of reductions in previously existing redundancies and in many cases even a lack of alternatives should an event occur. As a result, arrangements to improve production costs, such as just-in-time or lean manufacturing, have made their supply chain less resilient.

As underwriters, we need to understand our insured's supply chain flow, potential vulnerability and resilience. Note that insurance can help to mitigate some of the potential financial consequences resulting from a disruption subject to the physical damage condition, but it cannot address what in today's world is a key business survival element: a robust and holistic risk management process and approach to identifying the risks and the resulting sustainable reduction or mitigation measures. Even with the existence of insurance, it is very often difficult for an insured to achieve the same turnover level as before the event happened.

To become more familiar with and keep up to date with this topic, you will find a large number of publications dealing with supply chain risk management on the Internet. There is one publication that we would like to highlight here as it provides an annual analysis of the major disruptions that affected many companies during the year: the Supply Chain Resilience Report published by the Business Continuity Institute in the UK (see www.thebci.org). Given that the content is dynamic and changes over time, we will not reproduce the results here.

To sum up, to perform a proper exposure assessment, underwriters need to understand their customer's supply chain risk management approach/process. This will indicate how the customer identifies critical supplies and the resulting mitigation measures in place. These may include activities such as establishing and validating alternative suppliers, keeping appropriate levels of key stock or any other risk reduction or mitigation action. Remember that the BCP is generally not designed to prevent disruptions but rather to help ensure the survival of a company following a disruption.

4.2.12 Non-Damage Business Interruption (NDBI)

Traditional business interruption insurance has experienced increasing pressure for many years now. I can recall my discussions with some colleagues and risk managers back in 2006 about the need for a fundamental evolution and transformation. It is a fact that the current product does not embrace all the different needs of the market in general and customers in particular in terms of innovation and simpler coverage.

It is reported that Ludovic McLellan Mann developed the loss of profit approach in the UK in around 1899. While some adjustments were introduced in about 1939 and in the 1980s, business interruption insurance needs to cope with the current market environment and reality. Adaptation and evolution are the key words for this transformation, without disregarding the excellent work carried out by Ludovic McLellan Mann. What he developed at that time was not only an excellent invention but also a response to the needs of customers at that time. The current practice is to add an endorsement to the property damage policy, for example, in the US or to include a separate section in a combined policy (an approach mostly used everywhere).

Did you know that, in the 1960s, business interruption was a separate line of business in the UK? Underwriters used to have an underwriting authority for physical damage that may or may not have included business interruption. In addition, sometimes, the practice was to place the BI policy with another insurance carrier. Part of the reason was that business interruption insurance requires different skill sets from traditional property underwriting, which deals with tangible assets, such as buildings, machinery and stocks. While business interruption requires an understanding of the dynamics on the physical damage side (and the resulting business interruption inception risk), it also needs a strong understanding of the interruption risk: the supply chain vulnerabilities (dependency among the different production sites or from the suppliers or customers); the impact on the earnings of the insured and its ability to reduce this impact; and the speed of recovery to the situation before the event occurred.

As discussed in section 4.2.11 on supply chain resilience, many organisations face all sorts of disruptions, whether physical damage or not in their origin, which need to be addressed not only from a risk management point of view but also following an insurance solution approach. In this new solution, we are not promoting the concept of including the entrepreneurial risks that shareholders have to retain but suggesting new product offerings to cope with the current global and shared economy.

We believe that it is only a question of time before business interruption becomes a separate and more holistic line of business inclusive of risks and exposures. This change will also include the way in which we price business interruption insurance. Today, it is based on a factor of the property damage premium. Finally, the scope of cover will be broader and more inclusive of disruptions originating from material and non-material damage.

The question is not whether this transformation will happen but rather when it will occur. The pressure is increasing, and the market needs to prepare its evolution into this new method of business interruption insurance and decide how it will execute it as a win-win approach to ensure that customer needs are addressed while at the same time safeguarding the sustainability of the insurance carriers without jeopardising the profitability of the book of business. As a result of the described evolution, we have seen many insurance companies offering some "non-damage BI" extensions in an attempt to meet some of the customers' needs.

What is meant by non-damage business interruption? We could not trace any official or formal definition, but in general it is perceived as a way of protecting organisations when covered events cause a disruption to their earning ability irrespective of whether the event originates from physical damage.

Examples of such extensions that we have seen in the market range very broadly and widely from cyber coverage (physical and non-physical damage) to coverage for a number of disruptions, such as withdrawal of regulatory approval or the licence to produce; contingent business interruption due to non-physical damage affecting a key supplier; and blackout.[21] Additional examples include crisis management, waterway access, accidental interruption of services, extra logistics costs and probably many others that will be introduced into the market after the publication of this book.

In the meantime, due to the fact that there is no clear horizon indicating what is in scope and how to address non-damage business interruption in a sustainable underwriting way beyond a purely add-on approach, underwriters would be well advised to be very careful with these requests. Some actions include the following:

- Checking your organisation's underwriting policy for non-damage business interruption.
- Analysing the scope of cover very carefully; for example, what is the intention and how could it affect the overall coverage (claims, general and any other condition) under your policy, loss estimates, limits and deductibles?
- Regarding manuscript wordings, checking whether the operation clause has been amended to exclude the requirement for a direct physical loss.
- Making sure that, by adding these extensions, it does not become just an add-on approach since, without proper exposure analysis, you may face substantial unintended and unexpected losses.

4.3 Policy Wordings

Claudio Böttcher and Andy Baumli

This section will introduce you to a couple of principles to be borne in mind in relation to policy wordings.

4.3.1 Contract Certainty

In an attempt to end the "deal now detail later" culture, many countries have introduced the concept of contract certainty into their regulations. While this might not be the case in your country now, you need to become familiar with those countries that have already introduced it. This is relevant when you are crafting an international property insurance programme since local policies will have to be issued in accordance with those regulations.

As an example, in the UK, "the contract certainty project began in December 2004 with a Financial Services Authority (FSA) challenge to the UK insurance industry to end the deal now and detail latter culture. The industry took steps to improve the way it develops and agrees contracts ensuring that the Insured has greater certainty over what it has bought and the Insurer greater certainty over what it has committed to. Contract Certainty has brought operational improvements across the industry, reducing risk and improving service."[22]

The London Market Group developed the Contract Certainty Code of Practice. The current version of the Principles and Guidance can be found on the London Market Group website (https://lmg.london). Contract certainty is defined as follows:

> Contract Certainty is achieved by the complete and final agreement of all terms between the insured and insurer by the time that they enter into the contract, with contract documentation provided promptly thereafter.

Beyond regulations, the authors believe that contract certainty is the appropriate underwriting approach as it should help all the parties to achieve clarity before entering into the contract. First and foremost, we owe this clarity to our customers; second, it should assist in reducing potential claims disputes and litigation.

We have observed over the years, in a number of markets, the (mal-) practice of being already covered without having the final agreement on the policy wording. Obviously, this is not the ideal situation in the event of a claim. Hence, our appeal to the underwriting community is that, even in those countries where contract certainty has not yet been regulated, ensure that you adopt the same principles for the benefit of your customers and yourself.

4.3.2 Onus of Proof

As described in section 4.1 on property damage, earlier in this chapter, in a named peril policy, the insured must prove that the loss was caused by the insured perils. While, in today's environment, most policies are on the basis of all risks or a broad cause of loss, remember that, in such cases, the insured purely needs to prove that the property suffered loss or damage. The onus of proof is then on the insurance company to demonstrate that the claim did not arise from an excluded peril.

4.3.3 The Contra Proferentem Rule

This rule is also known as interpretation against the draftsman. It is a doctrine of contractual interpretation providing that, when a promise, agreement or term is ambiguous, the preferred meaning should be the one that works against the interests of the party that provided the wording, generally speaking the insurance company.[23,24]

Finally, there are cases in which the insurance intermediary drafted and introduced the policy wording. Once the insurance carrier has signed the wording, it is very often the view that either the insurance intermediary or the courts will probably consider it to be the wording of the insurance carrier, leading to potential disputes and litigation.

Remember that both the onus of proof and the contra proferentem principle are essential to ensure absolute clarity regarding what is covered and what is excluded. Together with contract certainty, you should be in a better position to avoid surprises when a claim arises. With the above in mind, let us now consider some additional aspects related to policy wordings.

4.3.4 Standard Policy Wordings

A standard policy typically has predefined wordings and includes standard terms and conditions. These wordings are generally applicable to a wide number of similar businesses. This is typically the case for householders, small and medium enterprises and, to a large extent, the middle market segment.

In general, it has been the practice in many countries for large customers (irrespective of how they are defined by each insurance company as commercial, global, corporate, etc) to issue manuscript wordings as described below.

4.3.5 Manuscript Policy Wordings

Opposite to the above, manuscript policy wordings are tailored specifically to particular customers in an attempt to make sure that they are more reflective of the particular coverage required. Manuscript policy wordings are required in situations in which there is a need, among others, to include a very particular type of coverage(s) or specific condition(s). The disadvantages are, and have been in the past, that manuscript wordings have been the cause of many claim litigations given the fact that, more often than not, they have not been aligned with the principles described above and the underwriting intention has not been clearly articulated.

One example will help to illustrate the issue: a local policy belonging to an international programme was issued in country A, which consisted of a local policy wording in the local language attached to a master policy wording from country B, which was translated into another language for the risks located in country C. An extension endorsement was added in the language of country A. Sounds complicated? You are right. Fortunately, the issue was corrected, but just imagine what the situation would have been had a loss occurred. Which conditions would have had to be applied and how much time would have been needed to settle any loss under such conditions, if at all?

Today, most insurance carriers have developed policy wordings that, while they are basically standard in nature, allow for some form of tailored solution.

Trade and Economic Sanctions

Trade and economic sanctions are restrictions imposed by governments or international organisations for political reasons. The goal is to maintain international peace and security.

It is possible that there are specific exceptions under which it is possible to engage. It may be possible to obtain a licence that would permit an organisation to carry out an activity that would otherwise be prohibited.[25] This will have a trade, economic or financial nature. It will generally target countries, goods or services and persons (comprising individuals, institutions, entities, charities, marine vessels, aircrafts, generally referred to as "specially designated nationals" (SDNs)).

Your organisation will have specific guidelines or instructions about the checks that you need to perform as well as the stage of the underwriting process (e.g., pre-binding checks). For international property insurance programmes, it may result in a country being excluded under the territorial scope clause described below. In addition, it is likely that your organisation will require the addition of a sanctions exclusion clause in the policy wording.

Note that trade and economic sanctions are serious regulations to consider. A breach of these regulations may result in financial fines and/or even imprisonment for the parties facilitating such a transaction. These may include the customer, the insurance company and the insurance intermediary.

4.3.6 Territorial Scope

The territorial scope in the policy wording will specify the geographical area that is covered as well as specific countries for which cover will not be provided. An example of the language used is "worldwide, but excluding …". In general, the aim of this clause is to exclude those countries or territories that are known to have politically or economically unstable situations. It may also include those countries where the insurance carrier may not have a licence to operate, the legal environment is extremely unpredictable or, as described in relation to trade and economic sanctions, a specific sanction has been imposed. As a result, when crafting the policy wording, it is important to ensure that the language also reflects the considerations given under the trade and economic sanctions and territorial scope.

4.3.7 Difference in Conditions/Difference in Limits (DIC/DIL)[26]

Andy Baumli

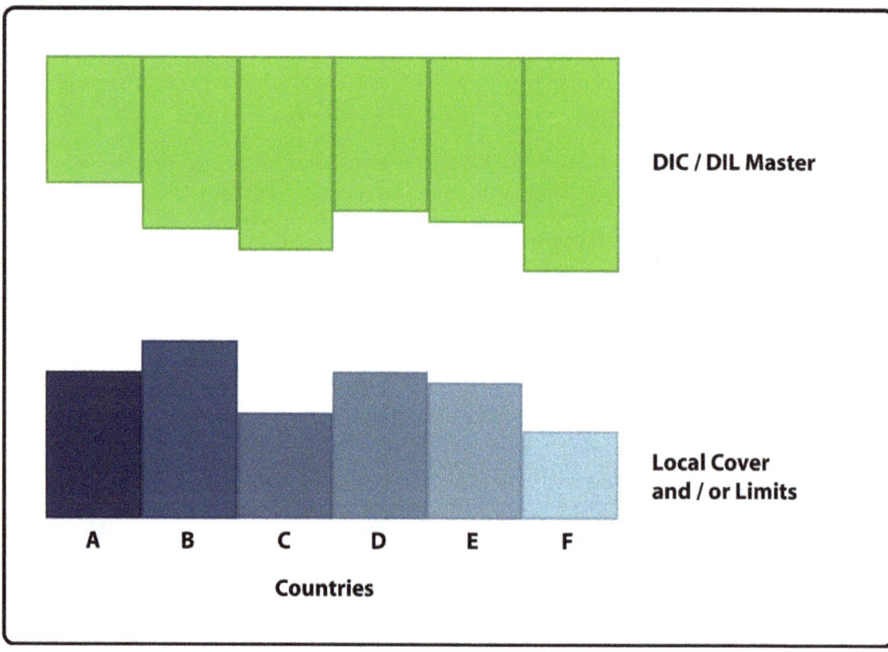

One of the key features of an international insurance programme is the master policy with special difference in conditions and difference in limits (DIC/DIL) cover. The DIC/DIL clause provides the master policy holder with peace of mind: an umbrella in the figurative sense, as shown graphically above.

We have discussed the variation of insurance policies above (Chapter 3). When instructing the local carrier (whether it is our own branch or a cooperative partner) to issue a "good local standard insurance policy", there are always gaps and differences in coverage and policy limits, whether intentionally or accidentally, which do not correspond to the overall intention of the purchased international property insurance programme cover.

Just imagine that you are responsible for all the insurance of your company group worldwide and a subsidiary faces an unforeseen claim that is not covered by the standard local insurance policy and there is no master policy with DIC/DIL in place! How would you explain to the stakeholders (the board of directors, senior management, shareholders, etc.) the lack of insurance coverage and the occurrence of a substantial financial loss for your company?

This extension of coverage requires that the master policy follows the wording under the local policy, and, in doing so, it will provide "difference in conditions and limits" coverage based on the scope of the local policy. In sum, the purpose of DIC cover is to protect against differences in conditions and gaps in the blanket of insurance protection, which, born out of necessity, a large company must place among many insurers, each using different fine print or conditions (Amax, 1978 U.S. Dist. Lexis 7150). The use of a DIC clause in the master policy context is to promote worldwide consistency with regard to terms and conditions. It is important for all the parties to understand the risks, appreciate the advantages and anticipate the unknown. It is the unknown that can subject the parties to costly claims. To avoid the consequences of the unknown, it is an inevitable requirement to review and understand the particular language of the DIC provision and to ensure that there is no risk of ambiguity. Creating clarity is the key to damage prevention!

From the previous explanations, it is clear that such a solution is intended for large corporations/multinational companies with operations all over the world. The DIC clause extends cover beyond what is typical of a local standard property policy. It is intended to supplement but not to replace the local policy, except for non-admitted countries. This coverage generally offers protection against major natural disasters, such as floods, storms, earthquakes and of course other perils. A master policy with a DIC/DIL clause may be less regulated than others, and insurers may not be required to file their rates or policy forms with insurance regulators. Thus, insurers are generally free to use whatever forms and rates they choose. Consequently, master policies vary from one insurer to the next.

Today, many global corporations also have operations within a European Economic Area (EEA) member state. One approach that may help to simplify EEA coverage is a freedom of services (FoS) policy, which is the same as a master policy in its nature. Based on my own experience, most master policies do not contain a coinsurance clause (underinsurance). This enables policyholders to insure their property for less than its full value without fear of a penalty for underinsurance.

Difference in limits (DIL) is a typical clause within a master insurance policy, related to the DIC clause, which may reimburse additional expenses greater than the limit established in the local standard insurance policy. For example, if the local policy pays out USD5 million for a flood damage claim, the DIL coverage in the master policy may pay up to an additional USD10 million if needed. The types of limits vary from policy to policy. Some contain both per-occurrence limits and aggregate limits; others contain only aggregate limits.

Reverse DIC/DIL

A "reverse DIC/DIL" is triggered when the local policy has broader insurance cover and/or higher limits than the master policy issued in the home country of a multinational client. A reverse DIC evolves to the programme underwriter; when a local policy grants coverage that is broader than the master policy, the broader coverage is imported into the master policy so that the master policy is actually extended to give the broader coverage up to the indemnity limits of the master policy.[27]

A good example of a reverse DIC/DIL extension is the earthquake cover in the USA, where fire following an earthquake falls under the fire peril, typically up to the local policy limit. In the case of DIL cover under the master policy in Europe with a sub-limit, the DIL loss would fall under the overall master policy limit and not the master earthquake sub-limit.

Underwriters most notably need to be aware of the variation across jurisdictions as undoubtedly inconsistent coverage will be afforded across jurisdictions. As a result, gaps must be fully understood. It is also a fact that, when the master policy is written in English and the local policy is written, for example, in French and issued by a French insurer, we must reasonably expect the terms in each policy to have varying meanings given the natural linguistic differences.

4.3.8 Financial Interest Cover (FinC)

In Chapter 3, we briefly discussed financial interest cover. To recap here, FinC extensions are in use when a parent company holds shares or any other financial interest in a local company. This extension will provide cover against the risk of devaluation of such shares or financial interest as a result of the local company incurring property loss or damage, meaning that the insurable interest of the parent company is the resulting devaluation of the shares or financial interest in the local company and not the loss to the local assets.

In addition, this extension is particularly applicable when:

- the global insurance carrier cannot issue a local policy because it does not have local representation;
- it does not have the applicable licence to insure the risks in the territory;
- local regulations forbid a local insurance carrier from reinsuring back to the programme insurance carrier; or
- the local regulations prohibit non-admitted cover as usually provided under the global policy DIC/DIL clause.[28]

The case M/s Adidas India Marketing (P.) Ltd. v. Income Tax Officer, ITA No. 1431/Del/2015 (29 July 2019), is probably the first court case involving the use of a FinC extension. There is quite a substantial amount of information on the Internet about this case, so you can become familiar with the details, outcome and different perspectives. Though this was a positive result for the insurance carrier, we would like to caution against placing too much confidence in the results of this case. There is no assurance that other regulators will make the same decision as the Indian regulator.

Given the rather complex nature of this aspect of cover, underwriters are advised to consider the inclusion of such an extension carefully, taking all of the above into account. An add-on approach is probably condemned to fail as it may not provide the desired effect.

4.4 Other Lines of Business

Customers or insurance intermediaries often request the inclusion of cover for other lines of business. While, for some, it might be a local practice to be included in the international property insurance programme, caution and proper consideration are advised. In particular, when a large schedule of values and exposure is involved, it is prudent for the relevant line of business to be at least involved in assessing the exposure properly and determining the terms and conditions and the related pricing. Not least, ensure that your reinsurance treaties will provide relevant protection should a loss occur.

Our general recommendation is to facilitate only the inclusion of other lines of business in an international property insurance programme for incidental business. This is "business written by an insurer which falls into a class other than that which it was formed to underwrite. This is permissible within certain laid down limits" (source: Insurance Industry Training Council, *Glossary of Insurance Terms*). As a rule of thumb, incidental business is usually expressed as a percentage of the location total sum insured with a maximum monetary amount, whichever is the lower.

Remember the principle stated earlier: we write what we know and we know what we write. The following are some examples of such requests.

a. Machinery Breakdown

In its simple form, "machinery breakdown provides cover against a wide range of losses from breakdown of plant production equipment, electrical equipment, boilers, pressure vessels, heating and cooling equipment, etc."[29] as well as the consequential loss (business interruption). The machinery involved can be very sophisticated (e.g., a unique and specific purpose design), and the time needed to repair or replace it and start up the plant could be relatively long. The age and type of the machinery, valuation, deductibles and BI indemnity period also play an important role in engineering underwriting.

There are countries like the US where it is common practice to include boiler and machinery insurance in a property policy. Nonetheless, our advice is still to include such cover only for incidental business unless specialised engineering underwriting is involved.

b. Inland Marine (Also Called Property in Transit)

> Inland Marine coverage – property insurance for property in transit over land, certain types of moveable property, instrumentalities of transportation (such as bridges, roads, and piers), instrumentalities of communication (such as television and radio towers), and legal liability exposures of bailees. Many inland marine coverage forms provide coverage without regards to the location of the covered property; these are sometimes called "floater" policies. As a group, inland marine coverage forms are generally broader than property coverage forms.[30]

While marine insurance provides insurance for goods that are conveyed over water, inland marine provides insurance for goods, materials and equipment when they are conveyed over land by truck or by train as well as when they are temporarily located in a third-party warehouse. In general, inland marine is written as a sub-branch/line of business of ocean marine insurance. The scope of coverage is also broader than traditional property insurance; for example, collisions while in transit and cargo theft are some of the additional perils included. It appears that, in countries such as the US, the practice is to include inland marine as an extension to the international property insurance programme.

It is our view that inland marine can be included in property insurance when dealing with small and incidental exposure and should be avoided when a large amount of transportation is part of the customer's operation. High-value products, materials or equipment should also be underwritten by the specific and exposure-related line of business with the relevant skills and expertise. From experience, we know that the frequency and sometimes the severity of inland marine losses, such as those related to collision and cargo theft, can destroy the overall profitability of an international property insurance programme.

4.5 Cyber-Risk

Do You Remember the "Y2K Case"?

> In early 1999, Australian multimillionaire entrepreneur and adventurer Dick Smith privately predicted that the Y2K bug would come to nothing and, as usual, he was essentially correct. An estimated USD 920 billion was spent worldwide combating the bug.

Underwriters around the globe were living in panic mode prior to the turn of the millennium. Y2K was then what the cyber hype is today. The media were full of theories, fears, predictions, scenarios, conspiracy theories and so on. We, as underwriters, had to deal with this problem on a daily basis, relying on reports, engineers and legal advisers to create a "Y2K Exclusion Clause". In the 1999 renewal season, many insurance companies enforced this exclusion clause in the contract. It goes without saying that corporations were not at all amused about this exclusion as they had to deal with the uncertainty of the Y2K phenomenon themselves. Certain insurers refused to enforce this clause, which led to them gaining substantial new business. We all know today what happened at midnight on 31 December 1999. All aircraft were still in the sky and all computers, electronic machines and installations continued working as usual.

More than 20 years later, "cyber" is the key word with ramifications. Government regulatory bodies and law enforcement agencies worldwide have taken numerous initiatives to tighten data security and protection. With the advent of COVID-19, the need for a cyber insurance policy has been realised by policyholders, brokers, insurers and agents. For example, in February 2020, the Californian assembly introduced a bill to make cyber insurance mandatory to process regulated and protected personal information for all state contractors. The rise in data privacy laws, such as the Personally Identifiable Information (PII) and the Health Insurance Portability and Accountability Act (HIPAA) in the US, the global standard, the Payment Card Industry Data Security Standard (PCI DSS), and the European Union's (EU) General Data Protection Regulation (GDPR), persuaded insurance providers to focus on cyber insurance measures. The increasing digitalisation has led to tremendous growth in the rate of cyber-attacks, particularly during the COVID-19 pandemic. Hence, complex governance requirements and regulations in data security are expected to drive the adoption of the cyber insurance market in the future.[31]

Cyber insurance policies are designed to mitigate risk exposure by offsetting recovery costs after a cyber security breach has occurred. Some of the common reimbursable expenses associated with cyber insurance coverage include:

- Business losses: These may include items covered by an errors and omissions policy in addition to monetary losses from business interruption, network downtime, data loss and recovery and so on.
- Investigation: These forensic investigations may be performed by a third-party security firm in coordination with the FBI or other law enforcement agencies.
- Lawsuits and extortion: These can include legal costs connected with the release of intellectual property and confidential information, regulatory fines and legal settlements in addition to cyber extortion.
- Notification and privacy: These cover required data breach notifications to affected parties, including customers, according to the law in various jurisdictions in addition to customer credit monitoring for those who may have had their information breached.

Some of the common cyber policy exclusions are:

- Bodily injury and property damage;
- Security standard exclusions;
- Previous acts;
- War, invasion, terrorism or insurrection;
- Laptop exclusion;
- PCI assessments and fines.

The above list of exclusions is not all-encompassing. Rather, it is a starting point for identifying some of the most common cyber coverage exclusions used by insurers. Cyber security professionals and risk managers should undertake a critical evaluation of the various types of coverage and exclusions contained within a particular cyber insurance policy to ensure that no unnecessary or unintended gaps exist.[32]

While new insurance products specifically include or exclude cyber risks, it is often unclear whether and to what extent existing policies cover them (Kirkpatrick 2015; Eling 2018; Siegel et al. 2018; Woods and Moore 2020). This unintended, implicit coinsurance leads to the so-called "silent cyber risks" of traditional insurance policies (Woods and Simpson 2017; EIOPA 2019). Silent cyber risks are defined as cyber risks that arise "from implicit cyber exposure within 'all-risks' and other liability insurance policies that do not explicitly exclude cyber risks" (Bank of England Prudential Regulation Authority (PRA) 2016).

Therefore, insurers face the challenge of identifying silent cyber risks in the various traditional insurance policies, in which cyber risks are regularly not mentioned or not explicitly included or excluded. Similarly, in traditional insurance products, cyber risks are often defined, but their subsequent handling is not clear. This makes it necessary systematically to identify, analyse and quantify comprehensively the existing but hitherto unknown cyber exposure. The aim is to take the individual components of existing silent cyber risks into account in the underwriting process. A detailed assessment of the existing silent cyber risks may entail uncalculated and difficult-to-quantify claim burdens for insurers (Willis Re 2017, 2018, 2019). At the same time, a holistic risk assessment should be carried out to reduce uncertainties by considering the existing accumulation aspects and developing adequate pricing approaches. As a result, insurers could include affirmative and comprehensive cyber coverage in their traditional insurance products. The topic of silent cyber exposure is also attracting the attention of insurance supervisory authorities (Pain and Anchen 2017; Eling 2018; Siegel et al. 2018).[33]

The topic of "all risk" vs "named perils" has already been discussed in Chapter 4.1 of this book.

4.6 Insurance Underwriting Capacity Deployment

One of the major strategic decisions of the senior management of any insurance company is the deployment of insurance underwriting capacity. Underwriting excellence remains paramount for company performance. Recent research from McKinsey's Journey Analysis, which examines leading commercial P&C companies over the past three decades, reinforces the reason for such high stakes. The analysis confirms what has been true for decades: there is significant variability among top insurance companies. What is more, operating results – more than capital leverage or investment returns – have the greatest impact on companies' overall financial performance.

Some insurers have a strong reputation for their underwriting capabilities – as reflected in their underwriting results – while others struggle to achieve consistent quality. When seeking to improve performance, it is important to recognise that underwriting is more than risk selection and pricing. It requires a comprehensive set of capabilities across hard and soft skills, qualitative judgements about future industry performance and rigorous portfolio management to avoid markets in which even excellent underwriting cannot compensate for unfavourable conditions. Underwriting performance is also influenced by exogenous factors, such as the business development activities undertaken with distribution partners to generate a consistent and attractive submission flow.

There is no "one-size-fits-all" formula for success. Underwriting operating models vary significantly based on industry, region, client size and product. Large corporate accounts have more bespoke coverage needs, so successful underwriting encompasses rigorous risk selection, with creative but prudent coverage design, and limits management. The most successful insurance companies are the ones with the insight and tools to deploy their underwriting capacity efficiently.

Digital technologies, evolving customer expectations and shifting demographics are among the top megatrends driving change in the next wave of the insurance industry. However, in terms of the long-term impact, the mainstreaming of alternative capital bringing greater capital options across insurance and reinsurance, when combined with the megatrends, may be more powerful in shaping the industry's future.

Recent mergers, joint ventures and alliances have further legitimised the view that alternatives are complementary to traditional insurance and reinsurance. These deals provided the acquiring companies with important capabilities and competencies that they did not previously have. For incumbent insurers and reinsurers, alternative capital offers flexibility and fluidity in capital deployment across cycles. Developing or acquiring alternative capital capabilities allows (re)insurers to be agnostic to specific instruments, even though they must navigate a complex mix of opportunities and risk. The threat of cannibalisation is real, but so too are the related opportunities to transform the current operations, adopt entirely new business models and strengthen the competitive positioning against non-traditional players, including tech giants.

For asset managers, alternative capital represents a shift in the way in which risk is viewed in the pursuit of returns. Asset managers are recognising that it is no longer sufficient to view these insurance-linked securities as solely financial modelling exercises but that, instead, they must embrace the details and economics of risk by merging classic financial bet placing with key elements of expert, risk-based underwriting. This is especially important as alternative capital makes its way into insurance products with long-tail exposures, such as cyber liability, which financial markets have not previously handled.

For both carriers and asset managers, a shift in perspective must occur. Asset managers must think and act more like traditional carriers, while carriers must adopt the mindset of asset managers. This fundamental sector convergence becomes especially interesting when viewed as new platforms for innovation in the industry. Imagine the possibilities of new business models, new forms of competition, lower-cost risk transfer and more insight-driven risk servicing as capital finds its most efficient path to customers and profitable returns – powered by the next wave of technology.[34]

As stated above, there is a very high capital base and underwriting capacity in the global insurance market. Everything therefore comes down to the appetite and strategy of an insurance company. We have seen and are still experiencing the following, among others:

- Companies moving into international insurance programmes (e.g., XL Capital – a Bermuda-based finance company – purchased Winterthur International through its sister company XL Reinsurance);
- Companies extending their portfolio through the acquisition of another insurance group (e.g., AXA purchased the XL Group);

- Companies expanding into other lines of business (e.g., marine, aviation, mining, the energy sector, etc.);
- Companies offering broader coverage in local markets (e.g., cyber inclusion and moving from "named perils" to "all risks");
- Companies moving into other insurance markets by opening subsidiaries and/or purchasing a local player overseas;
- Companies broadening their book of business by adding to their industrial, international and SME business.

With all these changes of direction in strategy, (re-)insurance companies deploy their capital explicitly, underwriting capacity into a new field of operation. Depending on the type of deployment, an insurer may acquire a distribution network, underwriting expertise and experience, local knowledge, market share and many other benefits. However, there may also be a downside when deploying underwriting capacity in unknown fields or perceived known fields. It has often been seen that insurers lack a full understanding of the extent of the necessary preparation for the far-reaching change in their risk appetite and its ramifications and consequences. All professional underwriters would agree that every target industry and every geographical risk needs fundamental underwriting skills and expertise. Experienced underwriters cannot rely solely on risk engineers analysing the risks. They must combine their expertise in tailor-made concepts and solutions to meet not only the needs of the customers but also the needs of the insurance company as well as its stakeholders (e.g., shareholders).

There is one other aspect to consider. All industries experience cycles of expansion and contraction, and this is particularly true of the insurance industry. Although no two cycles are exactly the same, insurance industry cycles typically last from 2 to 10 years or more and include phases characterised by the expansion and shrinkage of the insurance capacity deployed.

What is a hard market vs. a soft market? The characteristics of a soft market in the insurance industry include:

- Lower insurance premiums;
- Broader coverage;
- Relaxed underwriting criteria, which mean that underwriting is easier;
- Increased capacity, which means that insurance carriers write more policies with higher limits;

– Increased competition among insurance carriers.

Ultimately, these factors associated with a soft market affect insurers' bottom line as the insurance industry traditionally relies on a combination of insurance premiums and investment income to make a profit. However, as we have seen, the financial crisis, zero interest rates and volatile financial markets have a tremendous impact on the performance of an insurance company. At the end of the day, everything comes back to sound underwriting, which is for many insurers a strategic requirement: investment in underwriting skills and risk selection.

Now, how can all of these be applied? Given that you are satisfied with the risk, the conditions and the price, how much capacity would you put at risk, and what are all the weighting factors that determine the amount of USD you would put at risk? In my personal view, to respond to this question, "**it all comes back to your underwriting skills and experience, especially with international property insurance programmes**".

5

Programme Handling

Andy Baumli

The following programme handling chapter is linked to Chapter 3 ("potential types/solutions") and offers some ideas about how to set about structuring a programme. In contrast to Chapter 3, in which the possible options were explained, this chapter deals with the operational part once the customer and underwriter have decided which type of international property programme will be put in place.

One of my preferences in the underwriting process is to structure an international property programme based on the client's business profile and needs. That is probably the only area in the entire process in which an underwriter can show his creative skills: combining the hard factors with the immense possibilities for working out the best flow of communication, documentation, premium and claims and implementing the terms and conditions of the master programme on a worldwide basis. With the rollout, we can surely differentiate ourselves from our competitors and underline our capabilities to transform a solution into reality.

5.1 Setting Up the Programme Structure

The programme structure depends on the insurance concept and solution purchased by a multinational company. The following generic graphics should serve as an illustration of one of many possible structures that is commonly put in place.[35]

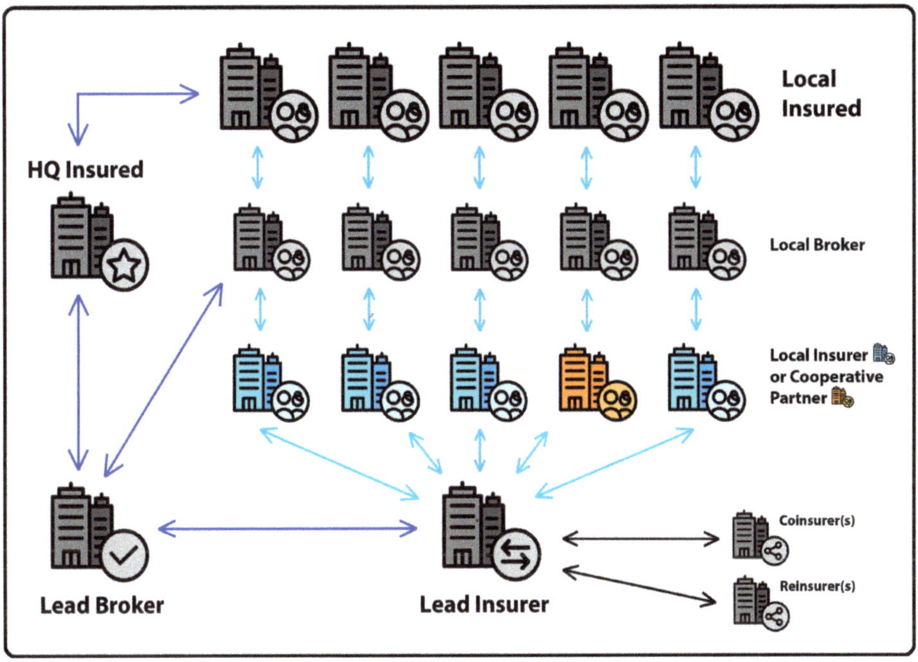

From an operational point of view, communication and systems play a crucial role in implementing an international programme. As easy as it is to understand how the generic flow of information, premiums and claims works, there are still a few obstacles to be aware of and to overcome. To start with, *"When dealing with people, remember you are not dealing with creatures of logic, but creatures of emotion".*— **Dale Carnegie**

Dealing with a programme also means dealing with people. An understanding of the cultural aspects as much as the linguistic topics is fundamental to an efficient and flawless implementation of the programme. This is not only the case within the insurance company but also applies to brokers and clients. How often have I seen that these points have been underestimated and therefore a smooth rollout has been disrupted?

Without a functional administration system, it is almost impossible today to handle a programme, especially a complex one. I remember that, in the 1980s, all communications, submissions and documents had to pass through our desks in the property insurance head office department in Zurich. We used solely telephones, paper and sometimes even the telefax machine. It worked at that time but was much, much slower and error prone. Fortunately, technological development allows us all to make use of the latest evolutions.

As we know, a system is only as good as its developers' conversion of the clients' and internal stakeholders' needs.

Very often, we anticipate that local contact persons have the necessary skills and offices have adequate processes in place. The work of the leading underwriter is not completed with the signing of the master policy. It is his responsibility to ensure that the local partners have all the information in hand to fulfil their tasks. This is an obstacle that we tend to ignore a little to the detriment of the implementation process.

5.1.1 Policies within a Property Programme

The following graphic[36] shows the link between the possible local policies and the master policy in the producing country within an international property insurance programme.

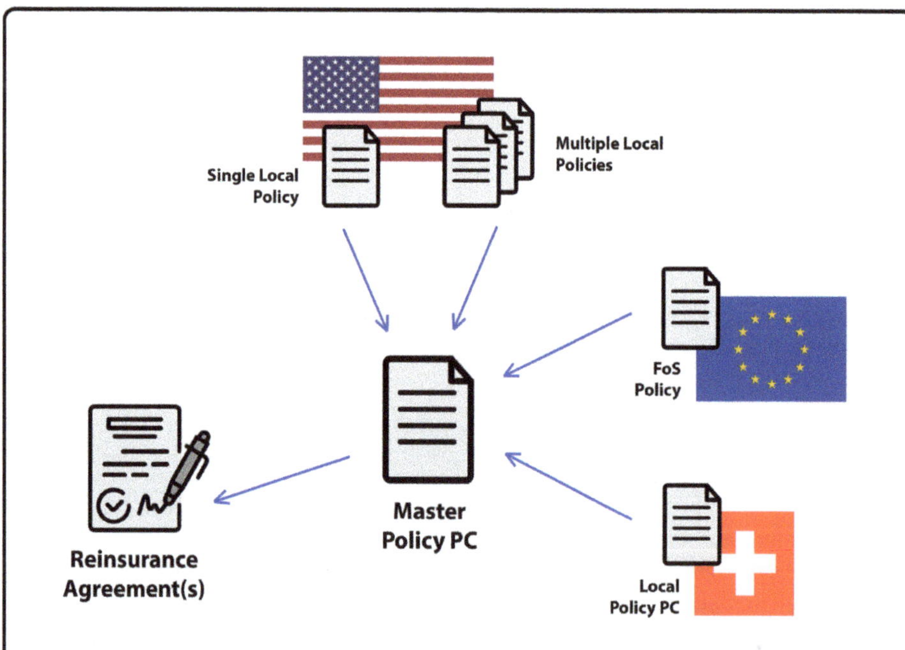

The structure of a programme should combine efficiency and effectiveness to achieve productivity. Therefore, **"Keep it simple!"**

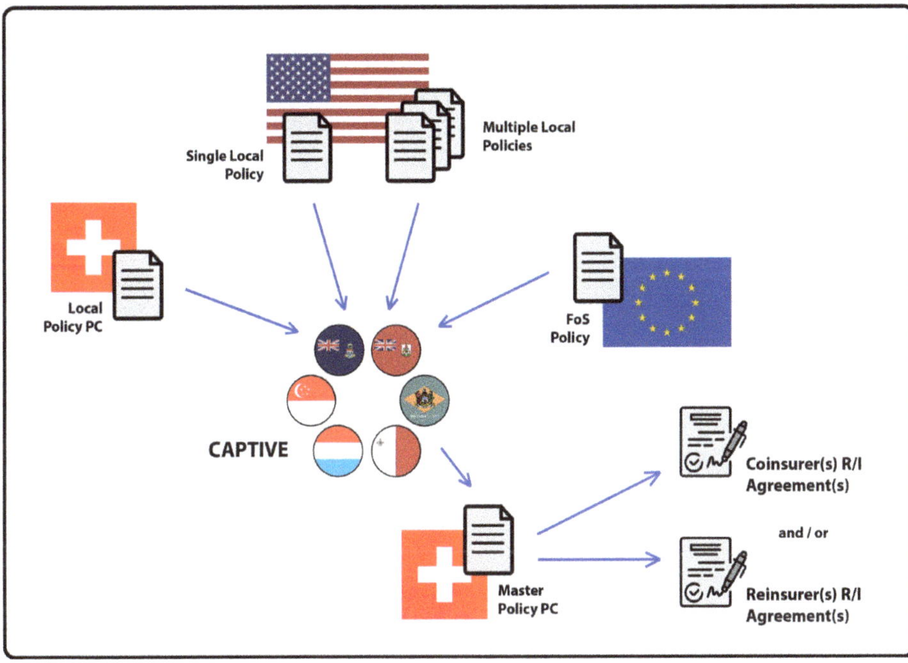

In line with Chapter 3.5, the structure of an international programme will change with the implementation of a captive solution, as shown above.[37]

The involvement of a captive in the programme structure demands an adjustment in the setting of priorities. The management company of a captive is clearly focused on the premium flow and will judge the performance of an insurance company based on its adherence to the promise of a smooth and timely premium flow. Any delay of premium income means a discrepancy between money inflow and money outflow. The net retention of the captive has to be protected by capitalising it through premiums, capital, capital interest and other income. Reinsurance premiums have to be paid to insurance and reinsurance companies on time, operational expenses have to be covered and investment strategies have to be realised with the premiums. The renewal of an entire international property programme may be threatened by the fact that the premium payment deadlines are not met to the satisfaction of the parent company. This sounds logical and simple, but I have often experienced a hiccup somewhere within the insurance company's network, which can jeopardise the entire implementation of a programme and its running. Phone calls from upset risk managers in this regard are not always nice but very understandable. The premium can only flow on the set deadline when the local policy is issued without delay on the inception date of the programme, and here we come back to the duty of the leading underwriter to ensure that the local underwriters are correctly instructed and have all the necessary information to complete the task promptly. The cooperation between the local client, the broker and the insurer (the "golden triangle") plays a crucial role and brings us back to communication as the key to success. Would it be wishful thinking for the programme's leading underwriter in the producing country, the broker of the home country and the HQ of the client to inform, instruct and guide their contact person simultaneously in the programme network to avoid confusion and delays? I do not think so; over the past years, efforts have been made to integrate digitalisation to reduce the complexity of the administrative effort, to eliminate sources of error and to drive down costs. Self-built systems or purchased solutions support all the parties involved in one or another way in coping with the implementation and management of an international programme.

Some insurance companies have even outsourced all their administration matters to a third party, which not only has more experience and expertise but also the technical tools to manage the administration in a cost-effective manner.

Local Policy – Fronting Policy – Admitted (FinC)

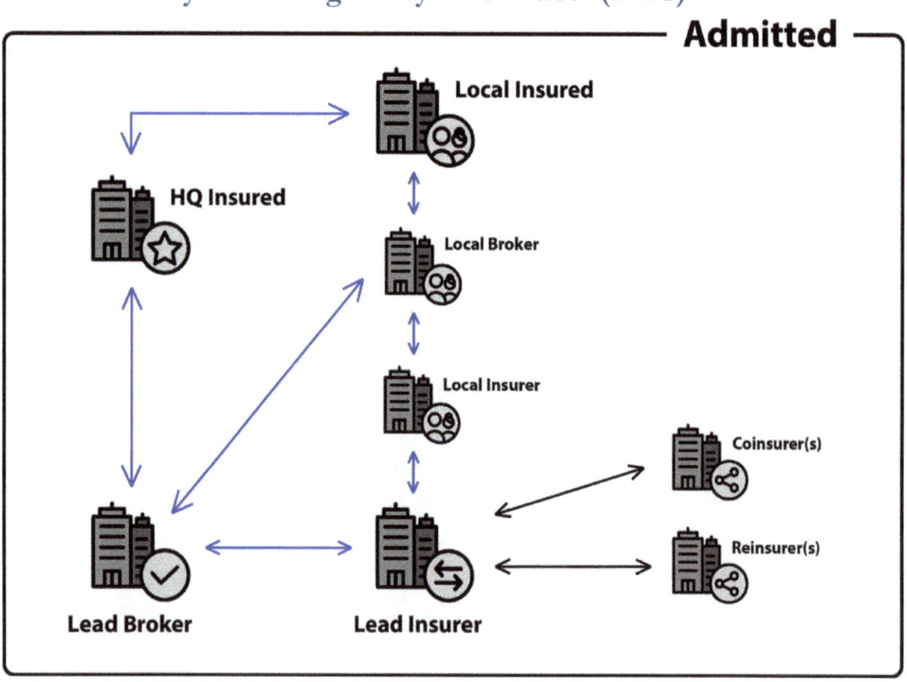

Local Policy – Fronting Policy – Non-admitted (FinC)[38]

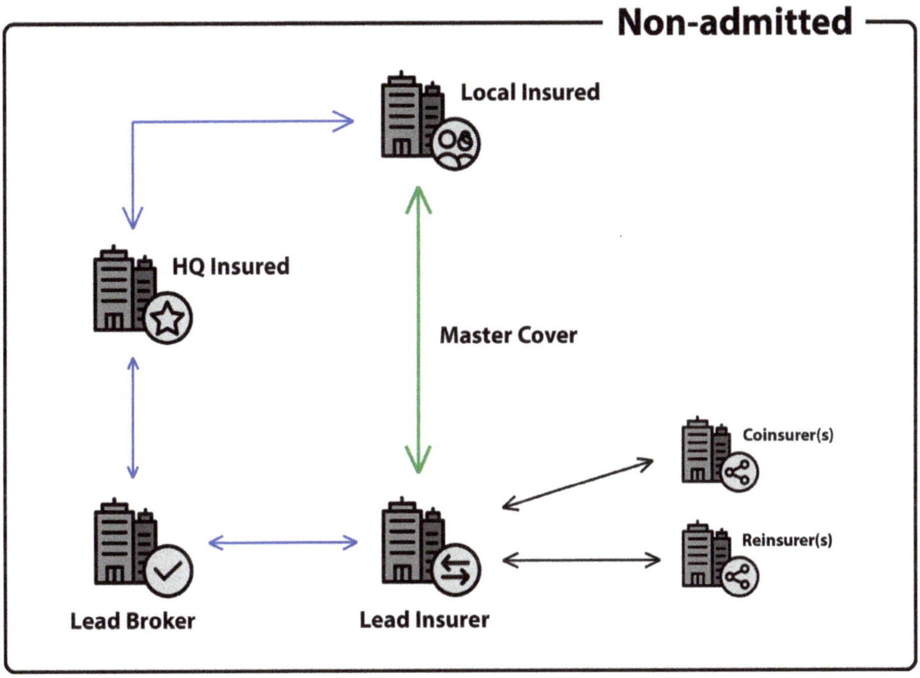

Whether we prefer one variant to another depends on the client company's worldwide setting as well as on the insurance network capabilities. Often, in some countries, there are just small sales offices, which need just basic local standard cover and little servicing. The question would then arise of whether it makes sense to integrate the branch into the programme and/or whether it can be covered legally on a non-admitted basis, as outlined in Chapter 4.3 (FinC). These options may also be suitable for circumstances in which clients have adopted a lower level of financial integration or a less centralised regime of risk assessment and management.

As mentioned earlier in this book, the possible choice of "local policies vs. fronting policies/admitted vs non-admitted" reflects not only the profile and needs of the client but also the legal ramifications. Locally admitted policies may be issued by a local carrier or a strategic service partner; in any case, the leading underwriter in the producing country has to ensure the handling requirements for taxes, levies and fees imposed locally.

FOS Policy[39]

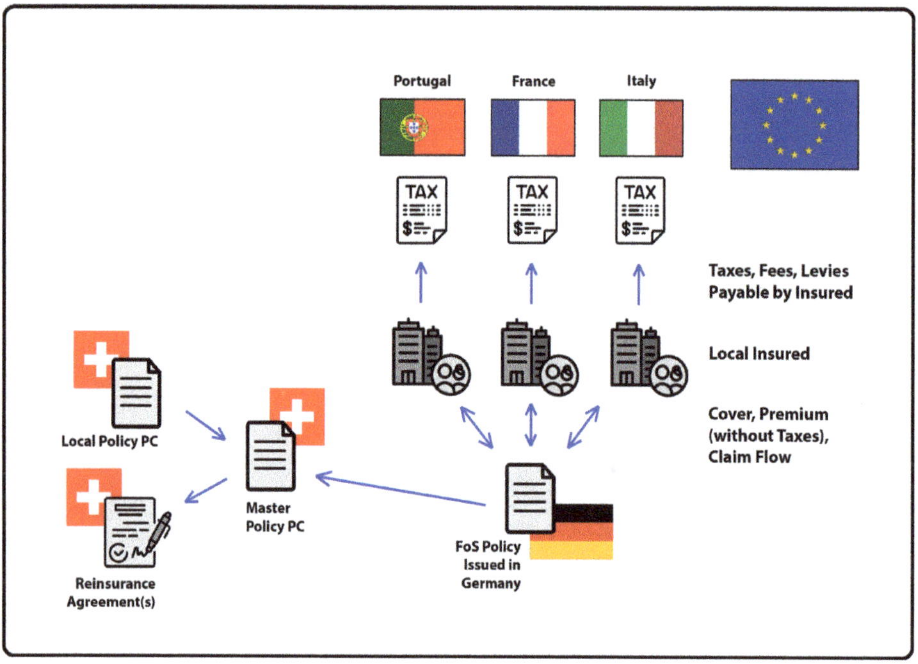

Through the application of a freedom of service (FOS) licence, insurance companies are able to offer insurance coverage within the European Union (EU) and the European Economic Area (EEA), as illustrated above. They must:

- Have the ability to provide admitted cover for 28 EU and 3 EEA countries;
- Be compliant with country-specific tax and compulsory insurance rules;
- Ensure full adherence to the local tax legislation, with central co-ordination of the insurance premium tax (IPT) transfer.

Key Features

- The Swiss master policy governs the global international programme;
- The FoS master policy governs EEA countries and is managed centrally in one EU country (in Germany in this example);
- Payment may be made in CHF, EUR, GBP or USD and can be handled via local collection or central premium collection;
- Taxes, levies, fees and so on must be paid locally on the allocated premium to the local tax authority;
- An FoS policy can employ DIC/DIL and ground-up approaches to address the risks appropriately;
- Non-EEA countries are managed on an admitted or non-admitted basis;
- The FoS Network Centre handles all the losses covered by an FoS master policy.

5.1.2 Claims[40]

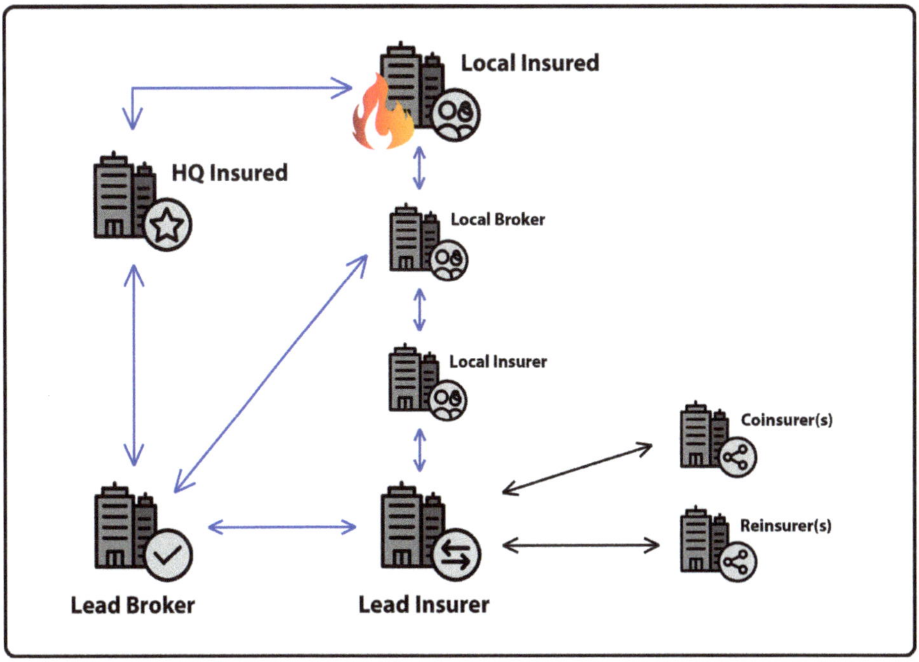

The communication flow must be part of the claims-handling agreement as much as the designation of the persons responsible for the entire claims process. Handling claims within an international insurance programme requires multilingual skills as well as in-depth experience in the national and international insurance markets. That is what sets a professional insurer apart. Whether the claim arises under the local, the FoS or the master policy or in combination is secondary. The most important point is to put in place, proactively and in advance, the forces of legal experts, claims adjusters and insurance specialists in a strong international network of reliable partners. Experience shows that a professional claims-handling agreement not only saves time and money but much more underlines the foresight and the endeavour to achieve smooth claims settlement and a fast cash flow, which clients expect from an insurance company as a given and by which they measure its overall performance.

5.1.3 Money Transfer

The money transfer follows the nature of the policies or cover issued and depends on the client's strategy and philosophy regarding financial integration: a centralised or non-centralised management regime.

5.1.4 Pricing

Do you remember? In Chapter 2, Step 3, concerning pricing, we explained the concepts of technical pricing and price to market. When dealing with international property insurance programmes, we need to ensure that all the aspects related to their cost are properly considered within the overall programme premium. Some examples are included as follows:

- Most of the large insurance groups have developed their own pricing tools. These tools consider not only the pure premium – the portion of the premium required to pay losses (attritional, large and catastrophic as well as loss adjustment expenses) – but also the loadings that have to be added to the pure premium for all the related expenses (direct and allocated, reinsurance costs and profit margin). In addition, for compliant programmes, a premium calculation for all the coverage aspects of the master policy will be established. These will include the admitted DIC/DIL premium and related local taxes, pure master extensions and coverage, among which will be included, for example, aspects like interdependency and FinC extension.

- When captive companies are involved, the allocation of the premium to the amount retained by the captive must be calculated as well.
- While insurance premiums have mostly been deregulated globally, you need to remember that there are countries where local mandatory tariffs are still applicable. You need to verify which of the countries involved in your programme may have a local tariff requirement. At this point, in property insurance, we are aware of countries such as Indonesia, Malaysia, Turkey and Switzerland. Very often, these tariffs refer to the size of the local risk, specific perils, such as floods and earthquakes, or even elementary perils and/or other issues, hence the need to check this information. In addition, there are the considerations explained in section 5.1.6: local insurance/reinsurance pools and/or market schemes.
- Large customers have often developed a large amount of claims information relative to their own company. It is not uncommon in situations like this for the pricing actuary to become involved and use this information to develop the pricing of an account since the amount of claims information is substantial and sufficient to develop the pricing structure. A good practice is to keep a fluent and interactive relationship with your actuarial pricing department as it will be able to guide and support you in cases like this.

5.1.5 Taxes

In many countries, insurance premiums are subject to taxation. This can take the form of value-added tax (VAT), goods and services tax (GST) or any other specific tax, such as an insurance premium tax, stamp duty or other levies. Furthermore, when a reinsurance cession is made for a local policy to an insurance or reinsurance company outside the country of risk, you will find that a reinsurance tax has to be paid in addition to the local taxation scheme in that country.

Compliance with local regulations has been a global trend for many years, and taxation is part of this trend. As with other similar topics covered within this book, compliance with local taxation requirements is a key component when setting up an international property insurance programme. Judicial developments in many countries in conjunction with increased collaboration among tax authorities underline our advice to take and follow local taxation very seriously.

How Do I Figure Out What the Country's Insurance Regulations and Premium Tax Rules Are?

The simplest answer is to google them. However, this is not the most professional method as many local issues might not be so straightforward and/or of a given complexity. The information found may also not be up to date.

Major insurers and broking houses have developed their online tools based on the data obtained through a global network of local insurance regulatory and tax experts in almost all countries in the world. The information is practically provided on a real-time basis. This information should help you and your customer to ensure greater alignment of the potential international property programme with the foreign insurance requirements. Remember that non-compliance with local insurance regulations and premium tax rules will have serious consequences not only for the insurance company but also for the customer and intermediary.

5.1.6 Local Insurance/Reinsurance Pools and/or Market Schemes

Besides risk management activities such as risk reduction, mitigation and control, one way in which the direct economic impact of catastrophic events such as terrorism, other social perils (strike, riot and civil commotion) or natural perils (earthquake, flood, etc.) can be mitigated or reduced is through the provision of government aid or insurance. Very often, some of these risks are undesired by the insurance market because the financial impact of the losses is too high to be borne by one insurance company or even by a number of insurance companies operating in a particular market.

In response to the lack of traditional insurance for certain perils in a number of countries, different solutions have been developed and put in place to fill this gap. In general, the approach has taken the form of setting up either a pool (insurance, reinsurance or a combination of the two, which can be state-owned pools or public–private partnerships) or a private enterprise (for example Extremus in Germany).

After the 9/11 terrorist attacks in the USA, a large number of pools and/or schemes were implemented around the globe. The list is too long to be reproduced here, but you can refer to the "Terrorism Pool Index 2019/2020" produced by Willis Towers Watson, which provides quite detailed information related to terrorism pools globally. Please note that terrorism pools are not the only pools that you need to be aware of when underwriting international property insurance programmes. As mentioned above, there are other pools/schemes related to other perils.

In a nutshell, you need:

- To check in which countries you need to consider a local pool or market scheme affecting your programme;
- Verify the potential gaps in cover that may exist between what your policy covers or excludes and what the pool or market scheme provides. It is important to make your customer aware of these potential gaps if they cannot be closed. Do not leave your customer with peace of mind when this is not the case.
- Be aware that, more often than not, if coverage provided by a local pool and/or market scheme is placed outside the relevant country, customers may be exposed to regulatory and tax examination. This may be the case following an incident affecting a customer's local operation.

5.1.7 Legal and Compliance

In Chapter 3.3 on compliant programmes, we explained how to set up such a programme. In section 3.4, we elaborated on how to figure out the country's insurance regulations and premium tax rules. In addition, in section 4.3 on policy wordings, we expanded on related legal/compliance issues, such as contract certainty, trade and economic sanctions, territorial scope and financial interest cover (FinC).

To enable underwriters to ensure legal and regulatory compliance with local country requirements, many insurance companies and broking houses have developed online tools based on data obtained through a global network of local insurance regulatory and tax experts in almost all countries in the world. A key note for you is that non-compliance with local regulations and premium tax rules will have serious consequences not only for your insurance company but also for the customer and the intermediary. These regulations involve not only specific local legal requirements (e.g., affecting coverage aspects) and premium taxes but also requirements related to the licence to operate as an insurance or reinsurance company, the applicability of non-admitted insurance and many others.

6

Reinsurance

Andy Baumli

This chapter deals with reinsurance, specifically facultative reinsurance and spot fac. as well as the importance of concurrency and credit risk control.

6.1 Excess of Loss/Fac. Reinsurance (Spot Fac.)

As far as I am aware, the first known excess coverage in the US was a catastrophe policy placed by Hatford in London following the 1906 San Francisco earthquake. Until the 1950s, little layered insurance was written in the US, largely due to communication problems, the cost of facultative reinsurance transactions, the lack of expertise and the absence of available domestic markets.

The best way to understand ***excess of loss*** insurance solutions is to start with the source of this kind of insurance and have a look at the reinsurance practice. The fundamental difference between ***non-proportional*** or ***excess of loss*** and the more traditional ***proportional*** or ***pro rata*** form of reinsurance is that, with the former, there is no proportional sharing of the original risk and premium between the ceding company and the reinsurer. The cover provided by a co-insurer or a reinsurer is the protection against losses over and above an agreed figure or limit occurring within a specific account and is written by underwriters in ***facultative reinsurance (fac. R/I)***.

Have you heard of the term ***spot fac.***?

Spot Fac. Individual (Spot) Facility

Spot fac. is nothing more than the purchase of reinsurance to cover one location of a given risk. If there is a large schedule of locations, there may be one or two locations that do not meet the underwriting standards of the insurance company.

The most common placements are for:

- natural perils (e.g., earthquake, flood, storm, etc.);
- a single risk or an entire insurance programme;
- the key location of a programme when the sums insured and the policy limit are higher than in the other locations of the programme;
- a very exposed location where the activity of the operation differs from the rest of the programme.

Within the underwriting assessment, the conceptualisation and the structuring of an international programme are crucial to meet the client's needs. We know that. However, the same applies to structuring our own reinsurance requirements. Based on the insurance company underwriting capacity deployment rules, we have to take into account the amount that we are prepared to put at risk. Let us assume that we are able to write a programme of this type of risk up to a policy limit or loss estimate (as defined by your own company) of USD200 million and that the policy limit required by the client and broker is USD400 million. We therefore, of course, need to structure our reinsurance requirements accordingly to obtain the lead on this programme. In one of my cases, the client was operating in more than 50 countries around the world. The split of risk was between manufacturing plants and sales offices across the globe. There was also a requirement to provide a USD50 million earthquake limit for California. For the sales offices of their sizes, I imposed a lower limit of USD10 million; that was not the crux but the earthquake limit for California and the fact that the production plants in the individual survey reported different risk ratings and loss estimate calculations. On average, all the producing locations were within the USD300 million mark except the key location of the programme, which clearly needed a limit of USD400 million. The question was whether I should opt for a solution of co-insurance combined with reinsurance on a proportional basis or whether there was another solution. After reassessing the given situation, I chose the following solution:

- Policy limit for sales offices: USD10 million
- Policy limit for manufacturing plants: USD300 million
- Policy limit for key location: USD400 million
- Policy limit for earthquake in California: USD50 million

Reinsurance structure[41] put in place:

- Deductible client: USD1 million;
- Proportional lead with 60% on the first layer across the entire programme;
- Proportional co-insurance with 40% on the first layer across the entire programme;
- 100% lead on the second layer with 100% fac. R/I (spot fac.).

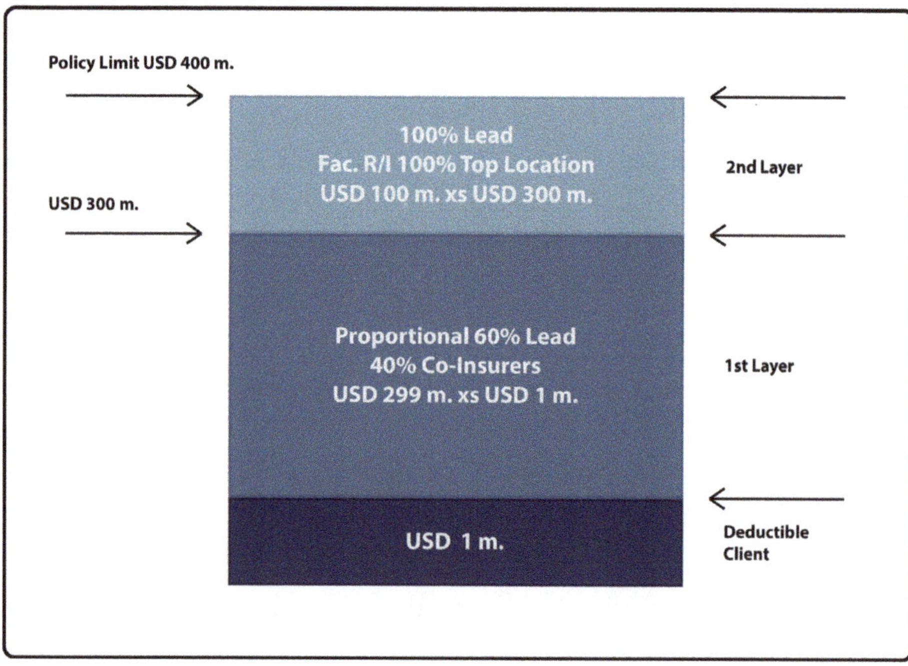

I am not claiming that this is the only solution, but it helped me to gain the lead on the international property programme. For layering reinsurance solutions, there are various first-loss scale tools, the most common ones being Salzmann curves, Lloyds scales, Ludwig, Swiss Re curves and PSOLD+. The basis of these first-loss scale tools may be TIV, PML or another, and it is important to remind the reader that there are *no consistent definitions for loss estimates such as PML, MPL, EML and MFL.*

The exposure curves play a very significant role in the pricing of property per risk excess of loss non-proportional reinsurance fac. R/I, especially in cases in which insufficient historical losses are available or the underlying exposure has changed significantly. The first research on this topic was undertaken by Ruth E. Salzmann (1963), in which cumulative loss cost distribution by percentage of insured value was introduced and it was shown that, for homogeneous groups of risks, such distribution was stable. The research was based on the claims data of the Insurance Company of North America (INA), and the fire losses incurred in 1960 were analysed as of 31 May 1961 (due to their short-tail nature, it could have been assumed that the losses were already fully developed at that time). The Salzmann's curves were reviewed later by S. Ludwig (1991), who applied the methodology to more recent data and made various practical suggestions.

The original Swiss Re curves, also called Gasser curves, were developed by Peter Gasser based on the data of the "Fire Statistics of the Swiss Association of Cantonal Fire Insurance Institutions" for the years 1959–1967. The curves are widely used by European reinsurers, and some recommendations for their application are available (Guggisberg 2004).[42]

6.2 ILS/Cat. Bonds

Insurance-linked securities (ILSs) are investment assets that are generally thought to have little to no correlation with the wider financial markets as their value is linked to insurance-related, non-financial risks such as natural disasters, other insurable speciality risks and life and health insurance risks, including mortality or longevity. As securities, some insurance-linked securities (mainly catastrophe bonds) can be and are traded among investors on the secondary market. They allow insurance and reinsurance carriers to transfer risk to the capital markets and raise capital or capacity. They also allow life insurers to release the value in their policies by packaging them up and issuing them as asset-backed notes.

The market for insurance-linked securities (ILSs) emerged in the mid-1990s as a mechanism for insurance and reinsurance companies to access the deepest and most liquid pool of capital available, the global capital markets. ILS/cat. bonds are clearly a well-established and valuable alternative to the traditional reinsurance solutions for natural perils. However, delving deeper into this topic is beyond the scope of this book.

6.3 Concurrency

Definition: "A concurrent condition is an act that the parties to a contract are under duties to perform concurrently and the act of each party is separately operative as a condition precedent".

Trust Is Good; Control Is Better!

6.3.1 What Is Concurrent Insurance?

Similar to reverse DIC/DIL (Chapter 4.3.7), there is also a danger in drafting a provision in a reinsurance contract, such as a concurrency of conditions clause, which may create a gap in cover exposing the insurance company to an unwanted risk, which can ultimately lead to a claim not being covered in full or the cover being extending beyond the underwriting capacity.

Court cases show the confusion arising when determining whether a provision in a reinsurance contract is a follow-the-fortunes provision or a follow-the-settlements provision. For an underwriter, it is rudimental to understand the ramifications of these two clauses. As courts have become more sophisticated about reinsurance, they now recognise that these are two different propositions. The follow-the-fortunes doctrine refers to a clause in a reinsurance contract stating that it is the reinsurer's duty to "follow the fortunes" of the insured as if the reinsurer were a party to the original insurance (source: www.Irmi.com glossary). The follow-the-settlements doctrine refers to the reinsurer's obligation to indemnify the ceding company for judgements or settlements paid in good faith in a reasonable and business-like manner that are arguably consistent with the terms of the underlying policies and the reinsurance contract. Under a follow-the-settlements provision, the reinsurer cannot refuse the good faith claims decisions of the cedent.

Concurrent causation is a method used in insurance claims for handling losses or damage resulting from more than one cause. The roots of concurrent causation stem from court rulings and opinions, which form a body of legal precedent that is useful when the parties in a dispute require the decision of a court.

In insurance, concurrent causation happens when a property experiences a loss from two separate causes when one has policy coverage and the other does not. Depending on the specific situation, the type of policy in effect and the state court in which disagreements will be heard, the damage from both causes is likely to be covered. Concurrent causation may also be a factor in liability insurance policies.

In summary:

- Concurrent causation refers to the identification of a loss that results from multiple causes, for instance a wind storm that causes roof damage that then leads to rainwater damage, which, in turn, causes mould.
- Many insurance policies today contain anti-concurrent causation (ACC) clauses that protect an insurer from paying out for the same claim more than once but that can be detrimental to some policyholders.
- While common in property and casualty policies, ACC clauses are also found in liability insurance policies.

With a concurrent causation loss, the events that cause the loss may happen one after the other or simultaneously. Today, most insurance policies will include an anti-concurrent causation (ACC) provision.

Concurrent causation legal precedents resulted from California's lower-court decisions in the 1980s. These courts ruled that claims for damages from concurrent events were valid. The judgement stated that, if a covered hazard added to the losses from an excluded risk, the entire loss is claimable by the policyholder. As an example, an earthquake causes a split in the foundation of a home, and a candle falling onto the floor during the shaking starts a fire. The property has a policy covering fire damage but excluding damage from an earthquake. According to the court's ruling, the entire claim is valid.

Example

An example of concurrent causation could arise when a tropical storm hits a commercial warehouse. Strong winds cause damage to structures, while heavy rain causes flooding. The door leading into the warehouse lobby is blown open by high winds. Floodwater further damages the floor of the front lobby.

It is impossible to separate the damage caused by the flood from the damage caused by the wind. The building has a commercial property policy that covers damage from wind but excludes damage from floodwater.

Under concurrent causation, coverage benefits will be due to the policyholder.

Insurance providers disagreed with this view, claiming that the ruling increased their liability and costs. They also argued that the decision ignored the existing exclusion clauses. In response, the Insurance Services Office (ISO) and commercial insurers revised the wording in homeowners' and commercial properties' policies, adding anti-concurrent causation.

The added anti-concurrent causation wording excludes damage from listed perils even if a second, covered peril contributed to the damage. The exclusion also applies whether the two hazards happened at the same time or in sequence. Many commercial property policies thus apply anti-concurrent causation language to specific exclusions, including law and ordinance, earth movement, government action, nuclear hazard, utility services, water, flood, fungus and mould. Not all state courts apply concurrent causation. Instead, they determine which peril was the proximate or predominant cause of a loss. Returning to our warehouse example, if the court decides that the proximate cause was the wind, then the damage should be covered.

The doctrine of concurrent causation applies primarily to an all-risk policy, which covers a broader scope of perils than a named perils policy. A named perils policy covers losses from only those perils listed in the policy. However, a named perils policy may still contain wording for anti-concurrent causation.[43]

Key Elements:

- Concurrent insurance is when two insurance policies are held to cover the same risks over the same time period.
- Concurrent insurance usually includes a primary policy, with the second policy meant to act as excess coverage.
- Insureds taking out concurrent policies generally do so when they believe that a single policy cannot adequately protect against a particular peril.
- There can be issues with determining which insurer should cover losses, however, which can lead to the need for the court to decide who pays.
- Concurrent causation relates to property insurance, stating that a loss should be covered when two perils, one covered and one not covered, cause damage.

6.3.2 Concurrency of Conditions

To ensure that there is no gap in cover, limits and deductibles, a reinsurance contract must have a clause such as the following:

> CONCURRENCY OF CONDITIONS
>
> It is agreed that this Agreement will follow the terms, conditions, exclusions, definitions, warranties and settlement of the Company under the Original Agreement, which are not inconsistent with the provisions of this Agreement. The Company shall advise the Reinsurer of any material changes in the Original Agreement which may affect the liability of the Reinsurer under this Agreement.

6.3.3 Special Considerations

Concurrency concerns the similarity between the terms and conditions (what is covered, limits, etc.) in the original policy and the coverage under the reinsurance contract (to avoid a gap in cover in the case of a loss).

6.3.4 Concurrent Insurance vs. Concurrent Causation

Concurrent insurance is two insurance policies held at the same time. Meanwhile, concurrent causation is related to property insurance. This type of legal doctrine states that, when damage results from two or more causes, one of which is covered and the other is excluded, then the loss should be covered. Specifically, a loss caused by two perils, such as wind and flooding, should be covered since it is generally impossible to distinguish which peril caused which damage.[44]

7

International Networks

Claudio Böttcher

This chapter will provide you with a view about the importance of an international network, how to structure the required network to handle your international property insurance programme and the value of good communication within your network.

7.1 Structure

To be able to provide efficiently and effectively the services that are required when handling an international property insurance programme, the insurance provider must fulfil the following basic requirements:

- The availability of a dedicated team with the ability and expertise to handle a whole account view:
    - programme structure and design tailored to the customer's needs,
    - policy issuance in compliance with local laws, regulations and taxation,
    - claims handling, whether from local policies or DIC/DIL,
    - premium collection,
    - captive services,
    - risk engineering services;
- Real-time digital programme analytics (including policy information, premium collection, claims handling and payments, risk engineering location, etc.);

- An API solution to enable the integration of the customer's risk management systems with those of the insurance provider, thus allowing the transfer of account-relevant information.

7.2 Own Network

Large and global insurance carriers have developed their own network since the 1970s, when the first insurance programmes were put into practice. In general, these networks are a combination of the local subsidiaries and an agreed number of local partners in the countries where they lack local representation. The size of these networks has increased over the last decades, and many of these insurance carriers are able to provide a holistic insurance solution in over 200 countries.

There is an amazing structure supporting the handling of international insurance programmes, including but not limited to partner management through regional hubs and specially designed systems to coordinate policy issuance and premium collection. Given the importance of compliance these days, these companies have developed systems to help make these programmes compliant with local regulations by providing country-specific information, such as whether non-admitted insurance is allowed, taxes related to DIC/DIL premiums and local taxation.

7.3 Third-Party Independent Networks

There might be situations in which your customer requires an international property insurance programme solution and the insurance carrier that you work for does not have the network structure necessary to deliver such a solution. This raises the question: "Now what shall I do?" In the absence of such a network, you may well have to decline the submission and miss the business opportunity given the lack of the required capabilities.

As a result, we initiated research to look for a proposal or solution to help you to overcome this problem, and we came across the following option. As precautionary advice, if you decide to take this option, we believe that you will need to analyse the case in much more detail.

As a minimum, you need to validate and analyse:

- The cost/benefit of that individual transaction;
- The need to build a relationship with this network to help you understand the services that it can or cannot provide you with in this particular case.

We are mentioning this potential alternative to avoid leaving you without any possible solution.

According to the information on the International Network for Insurance (INI) website: "INI was established in 1979. INI is a network of market leading insurance companies located in 150+ countries, across all continents. These partners work together to provide commercial and industrial insurance to international customers and brokers worldwide."[45]

7.4 Communication

In its basic definition, communication is a process by which information is exchanged between individuals through a common system of symbols, signs or behaviour.[46] We would not be surprised if you are wondering why we are including this topic here. Let us elaborate the rationale behind this and why it is important.

Most, if not all, international property insurance programmes are complex in their nature. Please note that this does not necessarily mean that they are complicated. Like everything in life, we can either handle complex issues in a simple way or we can execute them in a very complicated way. The complexity stems from the fact that many parties are involved in such a transaction, not only within the insurance organisation but also very often within the customer and broker structure. This is not a complaint but evidence of how we, as humans, can sometimes behave in a complicated way.

You will be aware of the number of details that are involved in establishing a programme structure, from the sums insured, location address, aspects of coverage, limits and sub-limits, deductibles and premium amounts to specific customers' requirements. The list goes on and on, but what we want to highlight here is that, because of the size and amount of all this information, effective communication is the key to the successful handling of such a programme.

We have learnt the importance of communication from our empirical observations throughout the years as insurance practitioners. How often have we seen upset customers because of the lack of, delay in or incorrect policy issuance or delayed premium collection and claims handling? How often have customers moved their account to another insurance carrier because of the lack of proper account handling and servicing?

Wrong instructions from the producing underwriting office have led to innumerable errors in policy issuance and, by the same token, the failure to address issues that, from a pure common-sense point of view, look wrong and have not been addressed on the grounds of "we have received these instructions and so we proceed".

Communication (not only restricted to the insurance world) is always a two-way street. If something is not clear or does not make sense, our professional accountability requires us to check it. Good or bad communication will be reflected in our reputation vis-à-vis our customers and intermediaries and should not be underestimated.

Most insurance carriers are investing substantial time and money in addressing the importance of communication by improving their international programme standards and systems with the aim of minimising the operation of disruptive communication. A basic principle to follow is to ask yourself the following question: "Will my counterpart understand the meaning and intention of my message?" In addition, please consider that, when you are working in an international environment, there are substantial cultural differences and very often what is clear to you may not be clear to someone else. Precise, simple and clear messages are more effective than long written emails.

8

Risk Management

Andy Baumli

This chapter will provide an overview of risk management. It will explain the critical use of risk engineering information as well as the difference between business continuity management (BCM) and business continuity planning (BCP). It will also highlight their importance in our underwriting process.

Last but not least, let us talk about the main features of risk management, which are of course an essential part of the underwriting process. The quality of the risk determines whether a new account is accepted, the pricing, the conditions, the limits and the deductibles; we know that.

Based on my own experience, the management of a company often decides to purchase another company for strategic reasons/purposes (e.g., an economical scale of business, symmetries or to remove a competitor from the market) without considering whether the acquired assets meet the standard of the existing risk profile and quality of risk and whether they are exposed to natural perils. The risk manager of a company, when such a function and position is even established, is often left with the task of integrating the new portfolio into the current risk management programme.

Some years ago, when I was underwriting a new international property programme for a major company group in Switzerland, I was faced with exactly that task. To expand the existing product range, this Swiss company purchased an Italian company that was also operating and selling its products worldwide. With the acquisition of this company, it not only increased the assets, turnover and access to new markets and broadened the product offerings but also acquired exposure to earthquakes in California, which it did not previously have. The risk manager was suddenly faced with dealing with this change to the well-set-up insurance programme. The Italian company did not have the same high standard in its risk management approach, and therefore a need for immediate action arose. The existing insurance cover had to be adjusted not only to include the assets and turnover but much more to purchase EQ cover for California. With not much information on the quality of the risk and the real exposures of the subsidiary in California, a joint action plan had to be put in place between the risk manager, the broker and our insurance company. First, we engaged our risk engineer to visit and conduct a survey of the location in the USA. At the same time, seismological data and information had to be researched and collected to evaluate the earthquake exposure. Combined with the result of the risk engineering survey report, I had to work out with my business partners (the client and broker) the exact need for cover and the capacity that we were able and willing to put on the table. It goes without saying that, without the great support of our risk engineer, I would not have been able to provide the client and broker with an adequate solution. It is no drama to mention that, in the end, I had to purchase an excess of loss cover just for the EQ limit.

8.1 Risk Engineering

This brings me to another phenomenon in the underwriting process. A survey report provides an underwriter not only with a quality rating, which, as we know, determines the capacity that we can put on the line for the individual location, but also, much more importantly, the information needed to understand the operational process, plant equipment, construction, protection and, not least, risk improvement recommendations. With your hand on your heart, can you say that these reports are studied in depth by the recipients? Unfortunately, the focus is often only on the rating, which is just a summary of the findings and is human made. A professional underwriter must understand the importance of such a valuable input from a risk management point of view to assess and to understand fully the nature of the client's business, exposures and needs.

Based on Chapter 8, risk management plays a fundamental part in the assessment of a risk and an entire book of business and forms the underwriting philosophy and culture of the insurance company. It is no wonder that global insurance companies have expanded their activities in their risk engineering service offerings to underwriters and their customers to allow them to manage the exposures and perils in a thoughtful and professional manner. Proper risk management assists the underwriting process by setting an adequate policy limit and level of underwriting capacity deployment. Expect the unexpected, or, as Hermann Hesse once said, "you have to try the impossible in order to achieve the possible".

In this sense, I worked very closely with the risk engineering department of the insurance company that I worked for as it always provided me with data, tools and insights to help me make informed decisions that I could justify. The same applies to our customers in setting up their risk management strategies and supporting their management with the total cost of risk. In reducing risk and mitigating losses, we, as underwriters, support our customers in the sustainability of their business, especially in the environment, social and governance areas. The ongoing cycle of risk identification, risk assessment, risk insight and risk improvement is our daily business and is the basis of our formulation of tailor-made concepts and solutions for clients in line with our insurance company's risk appetite, underwriting rules and guidelines. Nothing works in a vacuum in the underwriting process!

I regard the claims experience in a submission as a fascinating aspect of the underwriting assessment as it mirrors the risk management performance and approach of a client. The nature, frequency and maintenance losses probably indicate a moral hazard (Chapter 2.2) or most often poor management and an interest in reducing and mitigating risks from the client's side. The origin of the insurance philosophy "one for all, all for one" clearly belongs to the past. Customer needs and requirements have changed over the past few decades. Individual solutions at the best price and with the best conditions are a must today and pose a real challenge for underwriters. Then again, we also have an obligation to the stakeholders of our company. Therefore, we cannot ignore possible moral hazards and/or poor risk management. To enforce the importance of participating in managing risks and exposures, there are various options for us to consider, such as declining to offer insurance cover, imposing higher deductibles, charging a higher price, providing lower limits and offering only the current value instead of a new value; this list is not exhaustive.

When I came across an account in which the claims showed a negative tendency, I would organise a discussion between myself, my risk engineer, the broker and the client to understand and figure out the reasons behind the claims experience. Was it just bad luck, a lack of care or just a lack of awareness? Such discussions often led to an increased awareness from the client's perspective of the importance of participating in the mitigation of the risks and not just offloading them onto the insurance company.

I am of the opinion that recommendations from risk engineers must be part of the insurance offer and followed through accordingly over a period of time defined between the parties. The written commitment from the client to setting up an adequate risk management programme surely underlines the willingness to contribute to the overall success of the property insurance programme.

8.2 Customer and Insurance Company Benefits

The customer and the insurance company benefit equally from the input in the form of a survey report and risk improvement recommendations made by risk engineers. These are no doubt a key source for the risk assessment of an underwriter and do not replace the duty to understand the risk and follow the full underwriting process. For the customer, the clear benefit is the written state of the existing risk management approach, in which there is still room for improvements. It must be in the interest of the client to avoid any disruptions to the business and to achieve the strategic goals of the company. Here, we, as an insurance company, play a very important role in supporting the client in meeting the set targets by managing the risks and exposures to the best of our knowledge and protecting the assets, turnover and growth of the company and most importantly the reputation of the client's brand name, not only before but also after a loss.

Clients and insurers may have common aspects to consider, such as the impact of fire, explosions, natural perils and other disruptions affecting the business and insurance policy, but sometimes you, as an underwriter, need additional information about other perils to which the client may be exposed, changes to the organisational structure or strategy or technological developments. It is not sufficient to engage with the broker and client once a year during the renewal season of the insurance programme.

Both parties can benefit from regular contact, interaction, communication and dialogue so that unforeseen changes and events are discovered before they disrupt the insurance programme. As already mentioned above, a fully implemented risk management programme reduces not only the loss frequency and severity but also saves claims expenses for us and insurance costs for the client.

8.3 The Difference between BCM and BCP

In the BI section (Chapter 4.2.2), you learned about business continuity planning (BCP), which is not to be confused with business continuity management (BCM). Some companies have adopted a BCM and others a BCP.

They might sound like two names for the same thing, but there is an important difference.

To provide a little theory, **BCP** should be developed and implemented well in advance for an enterprise to ensure its effectiveness, and **BCM** is a structure for the maintenance/management of the **BCP**. BCM helps organisations to cope with incidents affecting their business-critical processes and activities, from the failure of a single server to the complete loss of a major facility. ISO 22301, the international standard that describes the best practice for business continuity, states that there are four major components to successful BCM: **management support, business impact analysis, risk assessment and BCP**.

The first three components come together in the BCP. It details the scenarios that an organisation needs to prepare for and how it will respond to them. The goal is to stabilise the situation and allow the organisation to continue operating as efficiently as possible until the disruption is resolved.

The element of surprise is often part of an attacker's strategy; therefore, it is not uncommon for a disastrous attack to occur without any warning. For example, it is difficult to predict cyber and terror attacks, natural perils and events such as the current COVID-19 pandemic. Most incidents are unique, and organisations must have the proper plans to recover quickly, minimising their downtime. Without a contingency plan, the recovery from sudden incidents can take longer, if it is possible at all, and is very costly, not to mention the loss of reputation.

Let us be honest: when was the last time you asked about the existence of a BCM/BCP as part of your risk assessment? Would you know the BCM/BCP of your own company? Many years ago, I did not even know that such a thing existed. It was during one of our discussions with a client and a broker in respect of setting up an extensive worldwide survey programme that I came across it for the first time when our client mentioned that there was a fully fledged BCM in place. As surprised as I was, I was also very interested to learn more about the business continuity management of my client. This was easier said than done. As the data and information contained in the BCM are very delicate and of the upmost importance to the company, I and the senior management of my insurance company had to sign a non-disclosure agreement. The BCM was presented and explained to me and my risk engineer in the office of the CFO of the company; no copies were allowed, but I still remember how impressed we were with the professional structure and details of the processes and measures in place. This meeting, as part of my underwriting assessment, was of the greatest value; although I was not allowed to take notes, I felt very convinced and comfortable in taking the lead in writing this international property insurance programme. The effectiveness of the BCM was proven later in a claim, which could have been much bigger without it and especially without having implemented sound supply chain management.

8.4 Underwriting Considerations

Summarising the above, the key considerations for me as an underwriter are:

- Make your risk engineer your best partner;
- Communicate regularly with the client and broker;
- Challenge the survey report and risk improvement recommendations;
- Read the report to understand the risk fully;
- Clarify your understanding with the risk engineer;
- The underwriting capacity deployment relates to the established risk rating as well as to EML, PML, MFL and so on – the definition may vary from one (re-)insurance company to another;
- Do not just take the risk rating: use your common sense and expertise.

Conclusions

Expect the **unexpected** to **happen**.

Sponsors

HDI Global SE

HDI

Global solutions require global action

Acknowledgements

Claudio Böttcher and Andy Baumli would like to thank Roger Krelshem for his most valuable comments, insights and feedback throughout the process of writing this book.

We also send a great "Thank You!" to our families for believing in us and our project of writing this book and for supporting our endeavour.

References

01 Rosenbaum, Hugh, editor emeritus of Captive Insurance Reports, and updated by the authors. (n.d.). The Early Days of Captives.
https://www.captive.com/resources/captive-insurance-history/before-1985

02 Comerica Bank. (2017, 2 October). 5 Questions To Ask When Considering a Captive Insurance Company.
https://www.captive.com/articles/5-questions-to-ask-when-considering-a-captive-insurance-company

03 Landry, Karin. (2019, 10 June). Captive Insurance: Why or Why Not?
https://www.captive.com/articles/captive-insurance-why-or-why-not

04 State of Vermont, Department of Financial Regulation.
https://dfr.vermont.gov/industry/captive-insurance/advantages-captive-insurance

05 Colombik, Jeremy. (2019, 20 November). How Does a Captive Insurance Company Work?
https://www.captive.com/news/2019/11/20/how-does-captive-insurance-company-work

06 Munic Re. (2021). Record Hurrican Season and Major Wildfires – The Natural Disaster Figures for 2020.
https://www.munichre.com/en/company/media-relations/media-information-and-corporate-news/media-information/2021/2020-natural-disasters-balance.html

07 Ooi, Sharon Joanne. (2019, 24 May). Secondary Perils – A Misnomer for Mounting Risks. Swiss Re.
https://www.swissre.com/risk-knowledge/mitigating-climate-risk/natcat-2019/secondary-perils-misnomer-for-mounting-risks.html

08 Dutch News.nl. (2020, January 18). Despite Being below Sea Level, Most Dutch Not Worried about Future Floods.
https://www.dutchnews.nl/news/2020/01/despite-being-below-sea-level-most-dutch-not-worried-about-future-floods/

09 Adriano, Lyle. (2020, 30 July). Does "All Risk" Insurance Cover Pandemics? Insurance Business America.
https://www.insurancebusinessmag.com/us/news/breaking-news/does-all-risk-insurance-cover-pandemics-229316.aspx

10 Computer History Museum. (n.d.). Timeline of Computer History.
https://www.computerhistory.org/timeline/computers/

11 Wilding, Claire. (2019, 1 November). The Accountant's Definition of Gross Profit vs. the Insurer's Definition. Astonlark.
https://www.astonlark.com/news-and-views/the-accountants-definition-of-gross-profit-vs-the-insurers-definition/

12 Fruhlinger, Josh. (2020, 27 February). What is a Cyber-Attack? Recent Examples Show Disturbing Trends. CSO.
https://www.csoonline.com/article/3237324/what-is-a-cyber-attack-recent-examples-show-disturbing-trends.html

13 Allianz Global Corporate & Specialty. (2014). Global Claims Review 2014: Loss Trends and Emerging Risks for Global Business. https://www.agcs.allianz.com/content/dam/onemarketing/agcs/agcs/reports/AGCS-Global-Claims-Review-2014.pdf

14 Pankow, Kristine L. et al. (2014). Massive Landslide at Utah Copper Mine Generates Wealth of Geophysical Data. GSA Today, Volume 24 Issue 1, pp. 4–9.

15 Scarpati, Olga Eugenia and Benitez Mirela. Las inundaciones en la ciudad de La Plata. Su analisis en relacion con las precipitaciones durante las ultimas decadas del siglo XX. Geograficando. http://geograficando.fahce.unlp.edu.ar

16 Marsh & McLennan Companies. The 100 Largest Losses 1974–2013. https://www.marsh.com/jp/en/insights/research/the-100-largest-losses-1974-2013.html

17 Allianz Global Corporate & Specialty. (2014). Global Claims Review 2014: Loss Trends and Emerging Risks for Global Business. https://www.agcs.allianz.com/content/dam/onemarketing/agcs/agcs/reports/AGCS-Global-Claims-Review-2014.pdf

18 Association of British Insurers (ABI). Standard Wording. https://www.abi.org.uk/

19 Association of British Insurers (ABI). https://www.abi.org.uk/

20 Chartered Institute of Procurement & Supply (CIPS). Single Sourcing vs Sole Sourcing. https://www.cips.org/knowledge/procurement-topics-and-skills/strategy-policy/models-sc-sourcing--procurement-costs/single-sourcing-vs-sole-sourcing/

21 Swiss Re Corporate Solutions. (2016). Non-physical Damage Business Interruption. PDF.

22 London Market Group. (2019, 8 July). Contract Certainty Code of Practice – September 2018. https://lmg.london/document/contract-certainty-code-of-ptractice-september-2018/

23 The Free Dictionary. (n.d.). https://legal-dictionary.thefreedictionary.com

24 International Risk Management Institute, Inc. (IRMI). (n.d.). Contra Proferentem Rule. Definition. https://www.irmi.com/term/insurance-definitions/contra-proferentem-rule

25 UK Government. (2012, 3 August). Trade Sanctions, Arms Embargoes, and Other Trade Restrictions. https://www.gov.uk/guidance/current-arms-embargoes-and-other-restrictions

26 Own design.

27 Nutton, Howard. (2014, 17 August). Global Insurance – Reverse DIC Explained. LinkedIn. https://www.linkedin.com/pulse/20140817093952-58957922-global-insurance-reverse-dic-explained

28 Roberts, Harry. (2012). Global Programmes – Compliant and Financial Interest Clauses. In Riley on Business Interruption Insurance (9th Edition, Chapter 12.7). Sweet and Maxwell.

29 Bommeli, Max. (2000). Machinery Insurance. Swiss Re. PDF.

30 International Risk Management Institute, Inc (IRMI). (n.d.). Inland Marine Coverage. https://www.irmi.com/term/insurance-definitions/inland-marine-coverage

31 Markets and Markets. (n.d.). Cybersecurity Market (with COVID-19 Impact Analysis). https://www.marketsandmarkets.com/Market-Reports/cyber-insurance-market-47709373.html

32 Warhurst Law. (2020, 24 March). Cyber Insurance Coverage and Common Exclusions. https://www.warhurstlaw.com/blog/cyber-insurance-coverage-and-common-exclusions/

33 Wrede, Dirk, Stegen, Tina and Graf von der Schulenburg, Johann-Matthias. (2020). Affirmative and Silent Cyber Coverage in Traditional Insurance Policies. Geneva Papers on Risk and Insurance – Issues and Practice, Volume 45, pp. 657–689. Springer https://link.springer.com/article/10.1057/s41288-020-00183-6

34 EY Global. (2020, 15 January). Four Future Impacts of Mainstreaming Alternative Capital in Insurance. https://www.ey.com/en_it/insurance/four-potential-future-impacts-of-mainstreaming-alternative-capital-in-insurance

35 Own design

36 Own design

37 Own design

38 Own design

39 Own design

40 Own design

41 Own design

42 Hrevuš, Jan and Luboš, Marek. (2019). Exposure Modelling in Property Reinsurance. Prague Economic Papers, Volume 28, No. 2, pp. 1–26. https://www.researchgate.net/publication/330836785_Exposure_Modelling_in_Property_Reinsurance

43 Kagan, Julia. (n.d.). Concurrent Causation. Investopedia. https://www.investopedia.com/terms/c/concurrent-causation.asp

44 Kagan, Julia. (n.d.). Concurrent Causation. Investopedia. https://www.investopedia.com/terms/c/concurrent-insurance.asp#:~:text=Concurrent%20insurance%20is%20when%20two,over%20the%20same%20time%20period.&text=Insureds%20taking%20out%20concurrent%20policies,protect%20against%20a%20particular%20peril.

45 International Network of Insurance. https://www.ininetwork.com

46 Merriam Webster Dictionary. (n.d.). https://www.merriamwebster.com/dictionary

Disclaimer

DISCLAIMER AND TERMS OF USE AGREEMENT

The authors and publisher of this book/ebook and the accompanying materials have used their best efforts in preparing this book/ebook. The authors and publisher make no representation or warranties with respect to the accuracy, applicability, fitness or completeness of the contents of this book/ebook.

The information contained in this book/ebook is strictly for educational purposes. Therefore, if you wish to apply ideas contained in this book/ebook, you are taking full responsibility for your actions.

EVERY EFFORT HAS BEEN MADE TO REPRESENT THIS PRODUCT ACCURATELY AND ITS POTENTIAL. EVEN THOUGH THIS INDUSTRY IS ONE OF THE FEW IN WHICH ONE CAN WRITE ONE'S OWN CHECK IN TERMS OF EARNINGS, THERE IS NO GUARANTEE THAT YOU WILL EARN ANY MONEY USING THE TECHNIQUES AND IDEAS IN THESE MATERIALS. THE EXAMPLES IN THESE MATERIALS ARE NOT TO BE INTERPRETED AS A PROMISE OR GUARANTEE OF EARNINGS. THE EARNINGS POTENTIAL IS ENTIRELY DEPENDENT ON THE PERSON USING OUR PRODUCT, IDEAS AND TECHNIQUES. WE DO NOT PURPORT THIS TO BE A "GET RICH SCHEME".

ANY CLAIMS MADE ABOUT ACTUAL EARNINGS OR EXAMPLES OF ACTUAL RESULTS CAN BE VERIFIED UPON REQUEST. YOUR LEVEL OF SUCCESS IN ATTAINING THE RESULTS CLAIMED IN OUR MATERIALS DEPENDS ON THE TIME THAT YOU DEVOTE TO THE PROGRAMME, IDEAS AND TECHNIQUES MENTIONED AND YOUR FINANCES, KNOWLEDGE AND VARIOUS SKILLS. SINCE THESE FACTORS DIFFER ACCORDING TO INDIVIDUALS, WE CANNOT GUARANTEE YOUR SUCCESS OR INCOME LEVEL, NOR ARE WE RESPONSIBLE FOR ANY OF YOUR ACTIONS. THE MATERIALS IN OUR PRODUCT AND ON OUR WEBSITE MAY CONTAIN INFORMATION THAT INCLUDES OR IS BASED ON FORWARD-LOOKING STATEMENTS WITHIN THE MEANING OF THE SECURITIES LITIGATION REFORM ACT OF 1995. FORWARD-LOOKING STATEMENTS GIVE OUR EXPECTATIONS OR FORECASTS OF FUTURE EVENTS. YOU CAN IDENTIFY THESE STATEMENTS BY THE FACT THAT THEY DO NOT RELATE STRICTLY TO HISTORICAL OR CURRENT FACTS. THEY USE WORDS SUCH AS "ANTICIPATE", "ESTIMATE", "EXPECT", "PROJECT", "INTEND",

"PLAN" AND "BELIEVE" AND OTHER WORDS AND TERMS OF SIMILAR MEANING IN CONNECTION WITH A DESCRIPTION OF POTENTIAL EARNINGS OR FINANCIAL PERFORMANCE.

ANY AND ALL FORWARD-LOOKING STATEMENTS HERE OR ON ANY OF OUR SALES MATERIAL ARE INTENDED TO EXPRESS OUR OPINION OF EARNINGS POTENTIAL. MANY FACTORS WILL BE IMPORTANT IN DETERMINING YOUR ACTUAL RESULTS, AND NO GUARANTEES ARE MADE THAT YOU WILL ACHIEVE RESULTS SIMILAR TO OURS OR ANYBODY ELSE'S; IN FACT, NO GUARANTEES ARE MADE THAT YOU WILL ACHIEVE ANY RESULTS FROM OUR IDEAS AND THE TECHNIQUES IN OUR MATERIAL.

The authors and publisher disclaim any warranties (express or implied), merchantability or fitness for any particular purpose. The authors and publisher shall in no event be held liable to any party for any direct, indirect, punitive, special, incidental or other consequential damages arising directly or indirectly from any use of this material, which is provided "as is" and without warranties.

As always, the advice of a competent legal, tax, accounting or other professional should be sought.

The authors and publisher do not warrant the performance, effectiveness or applicability of any sites listed or linked to in this book/ebook. All links are for information purposes only and are not warranted for content, accuracy or any other implied or explicit purpose.

www.ingramcontent.com/pod-product-compliance
Lightning Source LLC
LaVergne TN
LVHW051050210926
848486LV00001B/63
9781782229018